Information and Communication Technology

The Essential Guide

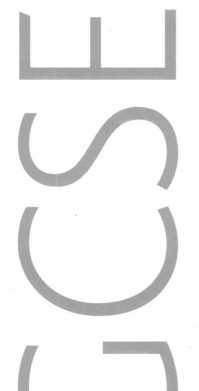

Flora Heathcote

Diane Spencer

Editor

Peter Sykes

Nelson Thornes

Published in 2010 by:
Nelson Thornes Ltd
Delta Place
27 Bath Road
CHELTENHAM
GL53 7TH
United Kingdom

12 13 14 / 10 9 8 7 6 5 4

A catalogue record for this book is available from the British Library

ISBN 978 1 4085 0584 7

Cover photograph: Strauss/Curtis/Corbis

Page make-up by GreenGate Publishing, Tonbridge, Kent

Printed in China

Picture acknowledgments

Alamy: page 20; 1.2F; 1.4M; 1.4N; 1.4P; 1.4Q; 1.6V; 4.1B; 6.3I; 7.1A; 8.1B; 8.2C
Author supplied: 3.4D; 7.2C
Fotolia: banner images for Chapters 2, 3, 4, 6, 7, 9; 1.1Ciii; 1.1Civ; 1.4L; 1.5R; 1.5S; 2.1A; 2.1C; 5.2G; 6.1Aii
Getty: 1.1Cii; 3.3C; 6.1Ai; 6.1B; 6.3J; 7.2D; 9.1D
iStockphoto: banner image for Chapters1,5 and 9; 1.1B; 1.1Ci; 1.1D; 1.4K; 1.4O; 1.5T; 1.6U; 3.5C; 6.1C; 7.2E; 9.1B
NASA: 7.3G
Photolibrary: 9.1A
Science Photo Library: 6.2E
5.2F courtesy of Erik Fairbairn, http://madracing.blogspot.com
7.2F courtesy of EyeTech Digital Systems
Microsoft product screen shots reprinted with permission from Microsoft Corporation.

Contents

Nelson Thornes has worked in partnership with AQA to ensure this book and the accompanying online resources offer you the best support for your GCSE course.

All AQA endorsed resources undergo a thorough quality assurance process to ensure that their contents closely match the AQA specification. You can be confident that the content of materials branded with AQA's 'Exclusively Endorsed' logo have been written, checked and approved by AQA senior examiners, in order to achieve AQA's exclusive endorsement.

These print and online resources together **unlock blended learning**; this means that the links between the activities in the book and the activities online blend together to maximise your understanding of a topic and help you achieve your potential.

These online resources are available on *kerboodle!* which can be accessed via the internet at **www.kerboodle.com/live**, anytime, anywhere. If your school or college subscribes to *kerboodle!* you will be provided with your own personal login details. Once logged in, access your course and locate the required activity.

For more information and help on how to use *kerboodle!* visit **www.kerboodle.com**.

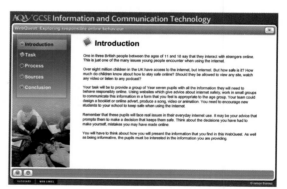

How to use this book

To help you unlock blended learning, we have referenced the activities in this book that have additional online coverage in *kerboodle!* by using this icon: *k!* .

The icons in this book show you the online resources available from the start of the new specification and will always be relevant.

In addition, to keep the blend up-to-date and engaging, we review customer feedback and may add new content onto *kerboodle!* after publication.

Welcome to a fresh look at GCSE ICT. This is an exciting new textbook to match the latest GCSE ICT specification from AQA.

ICT is an ever-changing subject. New technologies are continually being developed and soon become absorbed into everyday life.

The new content included in the book reflects:

- changes in the way in which people use the internet (for example using social networking sites, downloading videos and music)
- the growth of linking video, TV, music and games, based around ICT
- the growth of mobile technologies
- working together – collaboration between individuals and organisations.

It is a good time to study ICT because it provides the knowledge and skills which will help you to move into employment and Higher or Further education.

■ Examinations and Controlled Assessment

For GCSE ICT there are three assessment units. There is a written examination paper and two Controlled Assessments.

- Unit 1, which carries 40% of the marks, is a written examination paper.

There are two Controlled Assessment units which make up the remaining 60% of the marks. In both units you will be expected to be able to use a variety of software packages.

- Unit 2, which carries 30% of the marks, is called The Assignment: Applying ICT. For this unit, AQA will set two compulsory tasks based on up-to-date usage of ICT. You will provide the evidence to show that you have tackled and solved the two tasks.
- Unit 3, which carries 30% of the marks, is called Practical Problem Solving in ICT. In Unit 3 AQA provides a set of problems and you can choose one that you will enjoy doing. You can decide how to tackle this problem, but you will need to write a report and produce a portfolio of evidence to show what you did.

For research in Units 2 and 3, you will need to be able to access the Internet.

■ Supporting the new GCSE specification

This book has broken down the subject content into manageable chunks that match the AQA specification. The following features will help you to focus on key points and avoid common mistakes:

Objectives
These give you a clear indication of what will be covered in each chapter.

AQA Examiner's tip
How to avoid common mistakes and gain extra marks in exams.

Did you know ??????
Some of the more unusual but relevant facts.

Remember
Short tips and things to remember about ICT.

Activity
Short tasks to help you to broaden your knowledge.

Example
A short example of where ICT is used at home or in industry.

Case study
A focused look at real-life examples demonstrating ICT theory.

∞ links
A link to other parts of the book or a link to further reading and web sites.

Key terms
These are in blue when they first appear in the text. Definitions are given in the page margin and in the Glossary on page 137.

Summary Questions
Apply your knowledge in new situations before attempting the exam-style questions.

In this chapter you will have learnt
A round up of what you should know at the end of the chapter.

Boost your grade!
The essential extra knowledge for those intending to gain higher grades at GCSE.

AQA examination-style questions are reproduced by permission of the Assessment and Qualifications Alliance.

1.1 Computer systems

This section introduces you to computer systems. It looks at some of the **hardware** and software that make up a computer system and helps you to think about how to choose **input**, **output** and storage devices. ICT is used in communication and entertainment. The final part of this chapter looks at where and how it is used.

■ Information systems

One of the main functions of computer systems is to process data. There are three main stages involved in information processing: input, **processing** and output.

Look at this example of a supermarket checkout:

- The **input** to the system is the product code, taken from the number scanned from the bar-code.
- The input is then **processed**. The product details and price are looked up in the stock database.
- The **output** is a screen display showing product name and price. These details will also be printed on the customer's receipt.
- Details of new stock levels are **stored** in the updated database.

The relationship between these is shown in Diagram **A**.

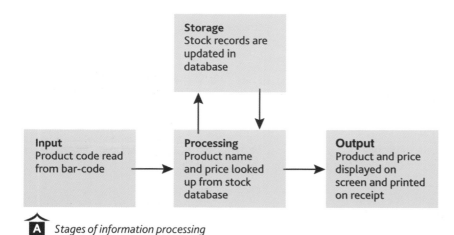

A Stages of information processing

■ Hardware 🅺

The physical objects that make up a computer system are known as hardware. Examples include a computer, a monitor, a printer or even a connecting cable. Hardware provides input, output, processing and storage **devices**.

Objectives

Be aware of the hardware and software components that make up a computer system or mobile device.

Understand a range of input and output devices and how they might be used.

Be aware of a range of ways of storing data and be able to suggest uses for them.

Be aware of communications and entertainment technologies and how they affect ICT systems.

Key terms

Hardware: the physical objects that make up a computer system, such as computers, monitors and printers.

Input: data entered into a system. Examples of inputs are bar-codes scanned in a supermarket, or key strokes entered by a typist.

Output: the action that occurs after an input has been processed. For example, the name and price of an item is displayed on a monitor following a bar-code scan.

Processing: turning the input into a useful form. For example, comparing bar-code data with a database to analyse which item it corresponds to.

Stored: information is kept for later use, for example information on the stock levels after the item has been scanned.

Types of hardware

The main component that makes a computer work is the **microprocessor**. The microprocessor is a silicon chip that contains the **CPU** (central processing unit). The CPU carries out all of the calculations that make the computer work. It is sometimes called the 'brain' of the computer.

Uses of microprocessors

Microprocessors are not just used in computers. They are used to control lots of devices, such as DVD players and washing machines. Mobile phones and games consoles also use microprocessors in order to function. They are an important component of office equipment such as photocopiers, but they are also used in industrial machines such as robotic assembly lines.

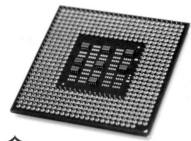

B   *The microprocessor acts as the 'brain' of the computer*

C   *Microprocessors are used in many different devices*

▪ Software *k!*

Software is the part of a computer system that you cannot see or touch. It is a program or set of instructions that the processor runs in order to carry out tasks that the user requires. There are two main types of software, **operating systems software** and **applications software**.

Operating systems are the software packages that control and manage the computer and its components. Computer programs such as word processors, databases or computer games are all examples of applications software. Operating systems are needed in order to run applications software.

The differences between hardware and software

- Hardware is a physical device that you can touch, such as a mouse or monitor.
- Software is program code that gives the computer instructions about how to operate. Computer programs are software.
- Hardware needs software in order to function.
- Hardware and software work together in computers and other devices that use microprocessors.

> ### Key terms
>
> **Devices:** pieces of hardware. For example, a monitor is an output device.
>
> **Microprocessor:** a silicon chip that contains a central processing unit, which acts as the 'brain' of a computer.
>
> **CPU:** central processing unit; the part of the computer that does most of the data processing.
>
> **Operating systems software:** controls and manages the computer. Examples are Windows, Mac OS and Linux.
>
> **Applications software:** computer programs that are designed to carry out specific tasks.

Components of a personal computer

Motherboard and central processing unit

The motherboard is the main circuit board in the computer. It has slots to plug in other boards and sometimes it has built-in sound and video controllers. Better-quality sound and video can be achieved if the computer has separate sound and video cards rather than using the ones built in to the motherboard. The CPU is a computer chip that sits on the motherboard. It carries out the main processing functions for the computer. Newer computers contain dual- or quad-core processors to make the computer work more quickly.

D *A motherboard*

Methods of processing

Interactive processing responds to inputs from the user. Most home computers work in an interactive way by responding to what you choose to do. An example of interactive processing might be in a computer game when decisions you make cause obstacles to be placed in your way.

Multi-tasking is when the computer is carrying out several tasks at once. It might be running a word processor and a spreadsheet at the same time as it is printing a document.

Real-time processing takes place straight away in response to input from the user. For example, if the number of TVs in stock in an online store is six and someone buys one, the level immediately reduces to five.

Online processing takes place when a computer is working via an Internet connection.

Multi-user systems allow many users to log in at once. For example, several customers may log on to the same website to look for cinema tickets. If you ask to reserve four seats, the computer will lock the records for those seats until you decide whether to buy them. It will then either mark them sold or return them to the system if you decide not to buy them.

Main/internal memory

There are two kinds of internal memory: **ROM** and **RAM**.

ROM stands for read-only memory. It contains instructions that are built in during manufacture, so that when it is inside your computer, it is read only. When the computer **boots up** it loads instructions from ROM, but the computer cannot write data to it.

RAM stands for random-access memory. This is used when the computer is operating and it holds programs and data while the computer is switched on. As soon as the power is turned off, data held in RAM is lost. Increasing the amount of RAM on a computer will help to improve its performance.

Input devices

The most common input devices used on a personal computer are a mouse and keyboard. The keyboard is mainly used to enter letters and numbers and the mouse is used to point and click. The keyboard also has keys for moving the cursor and can be used for shortcuts (such as pressing F1 for help). A separate section of the keyboard, called the numeric keypad, is useful if you are entering lots of numbers.

Output devices

The most common output devices are monitors, speakers and printers. The monitor is used to display what the computer is doing so that you can control the system using your input devices. If you need sound, it is produced by speakers. If you need to produce paper-based output, a printer is required.

Secondary/backing storage

Desktop computers need to store data and programs. For this they need storage that still holds data when the power is switched off. This is known as secondary storage or backing storage. The main backing store on a desktop computer will be its hard drive. Desktop computers will usually have drives for removable media, such as DVDs or CDs, but notebooks and other portable computers may not. They will also have USB ports that can be used for flash storage devices such as memory sticks. (See pages 21–22 for more on storage devices.)

> **AQA Examiner's tip**
>
> Know the uses for hard drives (main backing storage); memory sticks (small stores to transfer data between computers); DVDs/CDs (for permanent storage of files, for example music/photos).

Activity 1.1

What computer to buy?

Using the Internet, a computer magazine or an advertising leaflet, compare two desktop computer systems that might be suitable for use at home. The two computers should be quite different in price. Make a table like this one.

	Model 1	Model 2
Processor		
Amount of RAM		
Size of hard drive		
Other storage devices		
Monitor size		
Other features		

Describe what extra features the more expensive computer has and why they might be useful. For example, the more expensive machine might have a bigger hard drive. Why might that be a good thing to have?

Summary questions

1 Explain the difference between hardware and software. Give two examples of each.

2 Explain the difference between RAM and ROM and describe what each type of memory is used for.

3 Which of the following would use RAM and which would use ROM?

a Storing a word-processing program when it is being used.

b Storing the commands to start up the computer.

c Storing a music download which is being played.

4 List three ways that you could increase the performance of your computer.

1.2 The operating system k!

Operating systems software turns a set of electronic parts into a working computer. It controls the system hardware and software. It allocates memory and processor time to each process that your computer is running and it controls where your data is stored. Operating systems software also provides the **user interface** and useful tools such as file management software.

The user interface is the way that the user interacts with a computer system. It includes the input and output devices and the screen display that the user sees. The operating system also controls the type of user interface that the user sees on the screen.

Most personal computers use a graphical user interface or **GUI**. This is made up of windows, icons, menus and pointers, and so it is sometimes called WIMP. The user clicks on the icon or chooses from a menu and the computer responds to their choices. It is also possible to use the pointer to drag and drop items on a page. GUIs are quite easy to use and very versatile.

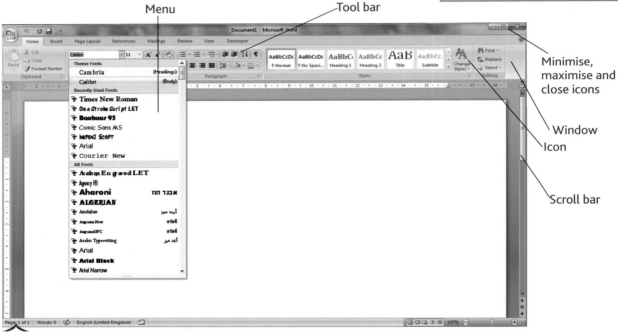

E *Graphical user interface, or GUI*

Features of a GUI

You can customise a GUI to suit your personal preferences. It is possible to change the size of the icons or even the icons themselves. You can add hyperlinks and hotspots to link to other pages or to external websites. You can alter the display options including changing the screen resolution and contrast. There are many other features of a GUI that you need to be familiar with. For a full list of features, see the Appendix on pages 131–136.

Menu user interface

Sometimes it is better to allow the user to choose from a restricted set of options. A **menu user interface** is a good way of doing this. Menu user interfaces are very easy to use and so they are often used in systems for the general public such as ATMs and information systems. Menu user interfaces work well with touch screens.

File and folder organisation

You will probably already be familiar with the folder structure of either Windows or Mac. A computer stores all files in folders. A folder can contain other folders (called subfolders), allowing you to organise all of your files and use many levels of folders.

Each file has what is called a **file path**. This is basically an address for the file that specifies exactly which folder it is stored in.

C:\Users\Public\Pictures\Sample pictures

G   *A file path*

The file path is in the address bar at the top of the window. The file path in Screenshot **G** is for the folder Sample Pictures, which is a subfolder of Pictures, which in turn is in the Public folder.

F   *This smartphone uses a touch screen and a menu user interface*

Key terms

Menu user interface: an interface where the user chooses from a restricted list of options.

File path: an address for the file that specifies exactly which folder it is stored in.

File extension: a code that defines the type of file. At the end of the file name there is a dot plus the extension, for example letter.doc is a document file called letter.

Activity 1.2

Find the file

Working in pairs, each of you should find a file on the computer, preferably one that is contained within a few subfolders. Write down the file name and the file path of that file (using the file path format as in the example in Screenshot **H**). Now swap file paths with your partner, and navigate to your partner's chosen file on the computer.

File extensions

All files have a **file extension**. A file extension shows what type of file it is – some common examples can be seen in Table **I**. Note that file extensions are usually three letters (occasionally four), and appear at the end after a full stop.

File names

There are some simple rules to keep in mind when naming files:

- Avoid full stops and special characters such as \ / < > * ? % : ". They are prohibited by some operating systems.
- Keep file names short. Some file systems do not recognise long names and will cut them short.
- Do not forget the file extension. When you double-click a file, the operating system uses the file extension to choose what program to open it in.

H   *You can see all of the files organised in folders and subfolders*

I   *File extensions*

Extension	Example	File type
.doc	letter.doc	word processor
.xls	accounts.xls	spreadsheet
.jpg	headshot.jpg	image

File sizes

Every file has a file size associated with it. A file that contains a lot of data will have a large file size. The file size is important because it will affect:

- how much space it uses on your computer hard drive
- whether it will fit on a portable memory stick
- how long it will take to e-mail to someone.

Typically graphics, music and video files tend to be very large, and because of this they can sometimes be troublesome to store or transfer. Word-processing documents tend to be small unless they contain many images.

Example

If you take a photo using a 7 megapixel camera, the photos could have a file size of about 5 MB each! If you have a selection of 20 photos that you want to give to a friend, that is $20 \times 5 = 100$ MB. You will need to decide how best to transfer the images to your friend.

Storing large files

Depending on how large your hard drive is, you may choose to store some files on an external hard drive. This is common practice for people who work with large files every day such as photographers, film and music editors. Some external hard drives are small enough to be portable, so they can provide a convenient way of transferring large files between computers.

Transferring large files

Many e-mail packages have a limit on the size of the attachment you can send. Also, the person you are sending the e-mail to may have a limit on the file size that they can receive. Sending large files can take a long time.

You can also transfer files using CDs, DVDs, USB memory sticks and portable external hard drives. However, obviously you either have to physically hand over the files or send them in the post. Typical capacities for these storage devices are:

- **CDs:** 650 MB
- **DVDs:** 4.7 GB
- **USB memory stick:** this is increasing all the time, but 1–16 GB is common
- **Portable external hard drive:** this is increasing all the time, but 100–500 GB is common.

Encoding data

When data is changed from one form to another this is known as encoding. This is often done with large amounts of data so that it is easier for the computer to use it. Many systems encode data, mainly for the following reasons:

- to make inputting information quicker and easier
- to make retrieving data from the system easier
- to reduce errors
- to reduce disk space required to store the file.

Encoding data on mail-order forms

Look at the following form for Collar Fast mail-order shirts.

Item code	Item description	Qty	Price	Total
SLWHT16	Slimfit white shirt size 16	1	£32.00	£32.00
TSWHT12	White T-shirt size 12	2	£15.00	£30.00

Collar Fast has many different shirt styles, sizes and colours. In the catalogue, every item has a unique item code next to it, as well as a simple item description. When a customer orders an item, they only need the item code, but the item description is also included on the form to double-check they have the correct code.

Collar Fast also accepts orders over the phone. Customers call up and quote the item code they want to order. The sales staff look up the item code on the system and read it back to the customer to check they are ordering the correct item.

Collar Fast stores information on all orders for five years. For each customer it stores only the item codes from the order rather than the full item descriptions.

Case study

Activity 1.3

How is data encoding benefiting Collar Fast?

Discuss how the use of encoding is used to:

a reduce errors

b make entering orders easier and quicker

c make retrieving item information quicker and easier

d reduce disk space.

AQA Examiner's tip

Encoding uses a simple code in place of a word or description (for example, F = female) which reduces the entry time and saves disk space.

Summary questions

1 Describe three jobs that the operating system does.

2 a Explain two advantages of using a GUI.

   b Explain one disadvantage of using a GUI.

   c Why would you use a menu user interface in preference to a GUI?

3 Rob has saved a photo in a new folder called PaintballingDec09 which he created in the My Pictures folder on the C: drive of his computer. What is the file path of this photo?

4 A 1 GB file containing a lot of images as well as text needs to be transferred. Discuss whether each of the following methods of transferring the file would be appropriate:

   a burning the file onto a CD-R

   b saving the file onto a USB memory stick

   c e-mailing the file to a school e-mail account.

5 For each of the following scenarios, explain which solution would be best:

   a Caitlin has just returned from a geography field trip. Her role was to take photos and now that they are back at school she needs to distribute the photos to the rest of her team of six. There are 100 photos in total, each about 3 MB.

   b Gareth has just finished taking photos on location in Greece for a UK travel magazine. He needs to send all of the photos to the editor as soon as possible. The photos were taken on a professional camera with very high resolution and the total file size of all the photos that he needs to send is 1.5 GB.

   c Alexa is organising a youth-club trip. There are 23 members attending, and she needs to send out a five-page Word document with the final travel and accommodation arrangements. There are two maps in the Word document, but apart from that it is all text and tables, so the file size is only about 1 MB.

When a computer is switched on it uses the data stored in ROM to boot up. Networked computers usually boot up to a screen that asks for a user name and password. When you log on, your user name will control what you see and what files and software you can access.

At the end of a session, it is important to close all of the programs that you have open and then log off. If you forget to close files before you shut down, the data in them may become **corrupt**. This means that the file might not open when you next want to load it. If you leave the computer and forget to log off, it leaves your files open and anyone who uses that computer after you can access them.

In some systems a screen saver is displayed if no key is pressed for a set number of minutes. It is possible to set the system up so that the screen saver stays on unless the correct password is entered. Once you have logged off, the computer should be shut down properly rather than switched off. Leaving your computer on standby for long periods of time wastes energy.

Key terms

Corrupt: the data in a file is unreadable. This can happen if the data is changed or damaged in some way so that it cannot be loaded by the original software.

Identifying ICT problems and solving errors

From time to time problems will occur with any computer. It is important to know what to do and when to call for expert help.

Freeze

Sometimes the computer may 'freeze' and stop responding to software commands. On most personal computers pressing the Ctrl, Alt and Del buttons together will allow you to close the package and shut the computer down safely. You may still lose any changes made since you last saved. Software freezes are more likely if the computer is low on RAM or hard-disk space. Having lots of packages open at once also makes a freeze more likely.

Error messages

Errors may also occur when you are working with software. It is important to read any error messages carefully and follow the instructions given. If software freezes or error messages occur often, the computer may need to be checked by a technician. If the problems occur with just one software package, it may be useful to uninstall that piece of software and then reinstall it.

Did you know ??????

A dialogue box is a small secondary window used to display information for the user. The simplest type is an alert that displays a message and requires an acknowledgement such as OK.

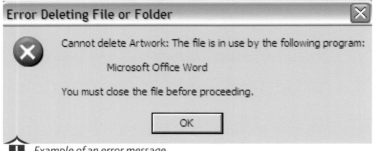

Error Deleting File or Folder ✕

Cannot delete Artwork: The file is in use by the following program:

Microsoft Office Word

You must close the file before proceeding.

OK

J *Example of an error message*

Storage space

If the storage space on the computer becomes too full, the system is likely to slow down and freeze more often. It is important to delete any files you no longer need. You can also archive files that you do not expect to need very often but do not want to delete. This involves copying them to removable memory, labelling them and storing them carefully. A removable hard drive that plugs into a USB port is a good way to increase the storage capacity of the computer.

Printers

Printers can also cause problems, especially if the paper is not loaded correctly. If the paper jams, it is important to switch the printer off before removing any jammed paper. Many printers have displays that show where the paper jam has occurred. New paper can then be loaded.

Obtaining help and support

Sometimes the error message will be enough to help you fix the problem, but in other cases you may need more help. Most businesses and schools have technical support arranged either through their own on-site technician or a support service.

If you need technical support, you will be asked for details of the problem. If it is a software freeze, you might be asked what operating system you are using and perhaps what other software you had open at the time. The technical support operator may be able to suggest some things that you can try. They can often talk you through a solution. If not, they will usually arrange a visit from an engineer. Some services have a system whereby they access your computer remotely and try to fix the problem or at least find out more about it.

If you are working from home and do not have a maintenance contract, it is worth doing an Internet search to look for help. Many bulletin boards discuss computer problems and may offer a simple solution. Software houses also have support sections on their websites and they may also offer support by e-mail. If you need telephone support you usually have to pay for it. Hardware problems will usually involve a trip to your local computer shop.

> **Remember**
>
> Store printer paper in a dry place. Damp paper is much more likely to jam in the printer.

> **Did you know** ???????
>
> The registry is a file on your computer that stores the important information about how it is set up. You need to be an expert to change registry settings safely. If you get them wrong, you can make your computer unusable.

> **Remember**
>
> Look carefully at an online help solution before attempting it. If it looks complex or suggests altering settings in the registry, then take the computer to an expert.

Summary questions

1 Raj is working on his computer at home and the screen display suddenly freezes. What should he do? What advice would you give him if this happens regularly?

2 How can you manage storage space to reduce the chance of a computer freezing?

3 a What is the most common problem with printers?
   b Explain how you can reduce the likelihood of this happening.

Input devices

There are a large number of input devices available. A few of the most common ones that you will need to know about are described here. In the Appendix on pages 131–136 there is a list of those not mentioned here.

Keyboards

Everyone who uses a desktop computer is familiar with a standard qwerty keyboard, but there are other types of keyboard too.

Ergonomic keyboards are bent slightly, a bit like a boomerang. They are intended to help people find a typing position that will not hurt their wrists.

A concept keyboard is divided into sections or has programmable keys. For example, in a restaurant, each key can be allocated to a product, so the waiter would press one button for a prawn salad and another for an orange juice. Concept keyboards are simple to use and avoid errors by restricting choices to a limited number of options.

K   *An ergonomic keyboard*

Mouse

A mouse is used to move a screen pointer and choose options on the screen. There are two main kinds of mouse: mechanical and optical. A mechanical mouse works by rolling a ball around a surface. An optical mouse uses a light beam instead of a ball. Optical mice do not need a mouse pad and do not get clogged with dirt in the way that mechanical mice do. For that reason they have become very popular.

Microphones

If you need to speak or sing into a computer you will need a microphone. Some look like the traditional microphones used on stage and others are built into headsets along with earphones. These can be extremely useful for call-centre operators as they leave their hands free to use the computer. Many laptops come with a microphone and web cam built in, so that video-conferences are easy to set up. Speech recognition software can be used to convert voice input into text that can be edited with a word processor. The software may still confuse words that sound the same but have different spellings.

Digital (video) cameras

For most people, digital cameras have almost replaced traditional cameras that use film. Once the photograph has been taken it is usually stored on flash memory inside the camera. This means that you can look at the pictures and delete those that you do not want or like.

You can then print the photographs or load them onto a computer to be edited. You can send digital photographs to other people by e-mail or to a mobile phone. You can also display them online on a social networking site or a blog.

Digital video cameras work in the same way, but they take many shots per second and they can also record sound.

L   *Microphone headset*

Touch screen

Touch screens are combined input and output devices. Wires are embedded in the screen and these sense when the screen is touched. Large touch screens are often used for information systems in public places. They are easy to use and do not need extra devices such as a keyboard or a mouse.

Touch screens are also used on many portable devices such as mobile phones. Some need to be pressed with a little stick called a stylus. Others can be operated with your fingertip.

M   *Touch-screen information systems are easy to use*

Magnetic stripes

Magnetic stripes are fixed to the back of plastic cards. When they are swiped through a reader, they input a limited amount of data. This might be an employee number that is recorded when the employee uses the card to open a security door. Credit and debit cards now use a chip and pin system, but they still have a magnetic stripe for older card readers. The stripe can also be used if the chip is not read correctly.

Sensors

You can fit a wide range of sensors to computers. The Nintendo Wii has specialised remote input devices that behave like other objects, for example golf clubs and guitars. They use motion and pressure sensors to sense the action of the player and reflect that in the game. Domestic devices such as washing machines and heaters contain heat sensors to control the temperature reached. Burglar alarm systems use pressure sensors to sense when someone has stepped into a particular area. Sensors are covered in more detail in Chapter 6, page 84.

N   *Game players use specialised input devices such as this steering wheel to make the game feel more realistic*

Automatic data-capture devices

Manual devices such as keyboards are inexpensive and very versatile, but they tend to be slow and it is easy to make mistakes when you use them. Automatic data-capture devices can be expensive to buy and set up. They speed up data entry and reduce mistakes, and so they are worth the cost if there is a lot of data.

Bar-code reader

Bar-code readers read printed bar-codes. A bar-code is a printed pattern of black lines on a white background. Each bar-code represents a number that is read when the bar-code is scanned. The bar-code reader has a checking facility. It does a complex calculation based on the numbers in the code. It then checks that the number matches a check digit, which is the last number of the bar-code. If it does not match, the reader beeps to tell the operator that the bar-code may be damaged. The operator then enters the number manually.

The number on the bar-code can be stored in a database where other details can be looked up. This will include the product number and other details, such as price and description, which are found from the database. Bar-codes are often used in library systems and supermarkets.

> **AQA** *Examiner's tip*
>
> A common mistake is to say that the bar-code contains details of the product. It does not. It simply contains a number that can be looked up in a database to find other details such as price and description.

OMR

OMR stands for optical mark recognition. You may have come across optical mark recognition sheets if you have taken a multiple-choice test. The sheet is printed with blocks and you choose your answer by shading in the correct box. The sheet is then scanned, and the scanner senses the position of the pencil marks. It matches them against the correct answer to calculate your mark automatically. Optical mark recognition is also used to fill in numbers at terminals that sell lottery tickets.

OCR

OCR stands for optical character recognition. It is used to convert paper-based text into computer text that can be saved and edited in a word processor. The paper-based documents are scanned to produce a picture of the document. Each character on the paper is then matched against a library of letter shapes to choose the correct letter. This is fairly easy on printed documents, but it is much more difficult with handwritten ones. This is because the letter shapes vary a lot and handwriting is joined together. Some systems use special forms divided into squares. You fill in each square with a single letter in block capitals. This reduces the number of possible shapes and it spaces the letters clearly. Passport applications use this type of OCR form.

Choosing an input device

Most data is still input into computers using a keyboard and mouse, but there are times when more specialised input devices are useful. When choosing an input device you need to think about the type of data to be entered, the user and the job that they need to do.

Activity 1.4

Form filling

Think about a business that involves lots of customers filling out application forms. Decide on the best two input devices to use and describe the benefits for both choices. Give a drawback for both of your choices.

O OMR sheet

P Passport application forms are read by OCR technology

Output devices

Monitor

A monitor or screen is still the most essential output device. It can vary in size from a tiny screen on a mobile phone to a giant plasma screen. The image on a monitor is made up from tiny dots called pixels and each one glows in a particular colour to make up the image. More expensive monitors have more pixels per inch of screen, giving a more detailed display.

Printers (laser and inkjet)

Most home users tend to use inkjet printers that work by spraying ink onto the page. They are cheap to buy and can be used for all types of printing, from text to photographs or even printable CDs. The ink to refill them is expensive and so they cost quite a lot to run.

Laser printers work in the same way as photocopiers. They use powdered toner rather than ink to make an image. The page passes through a fuser unit that heats up the toner and fixes it to the paper. Laser printers produce excellent-quality text and they print quickly. The cost to print each page tends to be cheaper than on inkjet printers, but laser printers are more expensive to buy.

Printers also have memory stores, called **buffers**, built in to them. The document is held in the printer memory store rather than in the computer's memory. This frees up the computer memory so that it can continue working at a good speed.

Speakers

Computers produce sound via speakers. Sometimes these are built in to the computer (internal speakers), which are suitable for system sounds (such as the beep that you hear when an e-mail arrives) and low-quality output. For music and high-quality sound, most people add external speakers for greater volume and sound quality. Earphones are tiny speakers and can be useful if you do not want to disturb other people around you.

Digital projector

If you want to produce a large image of a computer output, a digital projector is useful. The projector is connected directly to the computer and displays the image on a large screen. Projectors vary in brightness (measured in lumens), and a more powerful projector will be needed in a large room or a brightly lit one. The bulbs for projectors can be very expensive, and they are likely to fail if not shut down properly.

Plotters

Plotters are specialised printers. There are two main types. A pen plotter works by moving a pen left and right over a long strip of continuously moving paper. It can draw complex outlines but it cannot print large areas of colour. This type of plotter was originally used to print engineering drawings. A variation on this type of plotter is to replace the pen with a cutting blade which cuts through sheet material such as vinyl for signs. Smaller versions of these are also available for craft users who want to cut shapes from card.

Plotters are expensive to buy and they are usually bought by architects and engineering companies.

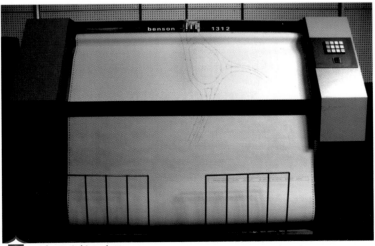

Q *A large inkjet plotter*

Activity 1.5

Which printer?

Look again at Activity 1.1 where you compared computer systems. Do some research into printers using the Internet, a computer magazine, or an advertising leaflet. Explain whether you think a laser or an inkjet printer is best for home use. Suggest some models that might be suitable for home use and give reasons for your answer.

Key terms

Buffers: temporary storage areas in the printer that hold the data waiting to be printed.

Control devices

Computers can be used to send signals that control almost any kind of electronic device. This can be as simple as a light or a buzzer, or something much more complex like a computerised arm. **Actuators** are used to turn computerised motors and other devices on or off or to adjust their speed. More information about control devices and the software used to run them is given in Chapter 6, pages 87–91.

Choosing an output device

In most cases there are not as many choices of output device as there are input devices. If you need paper-based output, you need a printer. You can choose what kind of printer, and that will depend on what kind of documents you produce and how many you print. Similar choices will apply to other types of output device. In general, more expensive devices will give you better-quality output and more features. The important thing is to decide whether those extra features are worth the additional cost for the job you need to do.

Summary questions

1 Imagine you are walking down your local high street. It has a bank, a supermarket, a newsagent and a launderette. Make a list of all the input devices that may be used in those businesses.

2 Describe what concept keyboards are and explain two different uses for them.

3 Which computer output device would be most useful for the following?

a Printing photos at home.

b Listening to a music download.

c Showing a summer holiday video.

4 You have the following input devices: keyboard, mouse, scanner. Which would be the most suitable to use in the following situations?

a To copy an old photograph onto disk.

b To select an item from a menu.

c To enter a set of exam results.

5 Describe the input and output devices that a cashier in a supermarket is likely to use, and what they might be used for.

1.5   Storage devices and media

■ Units of memory

All computer data is stored in binary form as ones (1) and zeros (0). The smallest unit of computer storage is a bit, which holds a 1 or a 0.

A byte is eight bits. A byte is very small, so it is usually talked about in terms of kilobytes (KB), megabytes (MB), gigabytes (GB), terabytes (TB). Each unit is about 1,000 times bigger than the previous one, so:

- 1 MB is just over 1,000 KB
- 1 GB is just over 1,000 MB
- 1 TB is just over 1,000 GB.

All types of memory and storage on a computer are measured in bytes, so a computer might have 3 GB of RAM and a 500 GB hard drive.

■ Backing up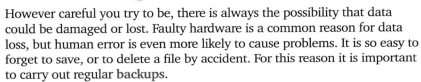

However careful you try to be, there is always the possibility that data could be damaged or lost. Faulty hardware is a common reason for data loss, but human error is even more likely to cause problems. It is so easy to forget to save, or to delete a file by accident. For this reason it is important to carry out regular **backups**.

How often data needs to be backed up depends on how often the data changes. Businesses will normally use mirrored server drives or duplicated servers so that many copies of their data are saved each time it changes. The type of storage media to be used depends on how much data needs to be backed up.

It is best to store backup media away from the main computer, preferably in a fireproof safe or in another building. You should also avoid storing media anywhere that gets damp or very hot or cold.

■ Choosing storage devices

Hard drives

The main storage device for desktop computers is the hard-disk drive. It stores a lot of data and is robust, fast and reliable. Hard drives are made up of metal disks coated with a magnetic material. They spin at a very high speed and data is read through a read-and-write head that moves in and out just above the disk's surface. Most hard drives are a type of local storage, and can only be used with the computer they are a component of. Removable hard drives are also available. These usually connect through the USB port. Their main disadvantage is that they take up a lot of room.

Optical drives

CDs and DVDs are known as optical media because laser beams are used to record and read data. CDs hold about 650 MB of data. DVDs can hold 4.7 GB or more. Optical disks have many uses. CD-ROMs and DVD-ROMs are ideal for delivering software or films. Writable CDs and DVDs are useful for transferring data and for backups.

Did you know ??????

Around 15 years ago a 2 GB hard drive was considered a lot for a server running a school network. Now far more data than that fits on a memory stick and servers will have several TB of storage.

Key terms

Backups: copies of data stored in case the original is stolen or becomes corrupt.

R   *Hard drives store most of the data on desktop PCs*

Did you know ??????

The distance between a read-and-write head and the magnetic disk of a hard drive is only a few nanometres. That is almost 10,000 times smaller than a human hair!

Activity 1.6

Reading and writing

Using the Internet or another good source of information, find out what the difference is between CD-ROMs, CD-Rs and CD-RWs. What are the differences between DVD-ROMs DVD-Rs and DVD-RWs? Think about where each of these types of CD and DVD would be used.

Flash memory

The newest type of memory to be developed is solid state memory. Flash memory cards (which contain solid state memory) are often used in digital cameras or MP3 players. Flash drives and memory cards are small and ideal for fitting into portable devices or transporting data from one place to another. Their size makes them easy to lose or damage, so they are less suitable for backup. Solid state hard drives are becoming more common and are used mostly in laptops because of their small size.

Memory sticks, or pen drives as they are sometimes called, are based on flash memory. They are fitted into a case with a USB connection. They can hold several gigabytes of data in a very small space and they are easy to carry around.

Magnetic cartridges

Magnetic cartridges, such as DAT tapes, are often used to back up servers. They can have a capacity up to 160 GB in a very small cartridge. Tape drives are mainly used for backup purposes.

■ Specialist storage media

Virtual memory

Virtual memory is a way of using the computer's hard drive to store some of the data that would be stored in RAM. This makes the computer behave as if it had more RAM and so it works faster.

Online storage

Online storage is becoming a popular method of storing data. Some companies offer small amounts of online storage free. They hope to encourage users to buy more storage space. Online storage has the advantage of being away from the main computer and so it is safer in case of fire or flood. There are security issues – you do have to trust the company that is storing the data.

Storing and sharing photographs

Some websites allow you to store photographs online. They may charge if you use large amounts of storage space. You can choose to keep the photographs private or allow other people to see them.

S *Flash memory cards are often used in digital cameras or MP3 players*

T *A memory stick or pen drive*

Did you know ??????

It is important to use storage media correctly. The media should be inserted carefully without touching the recording surface. When you remove the media, make sure the drive light is not flashing. The flashing light shows that data is being transferred and it will be corrupted if the disk is removed. Once you have removed the media, you should label and store it carefully.

◯◯ links

www.flickr.com allows users to store their photographs online.

Summary questions ✓

1. Why is virtual memory an advantage for computer users?

2. Describe two advantages of using online storage.

3. Which storage device is most useful for the following situations?
   a. Transferring small amounts of data between computers.
   b. Backing up data on a computer.
   c. The main computer storage.

4. Chris is working on a school geography project that requires large weather maps to be saved in addition to text and graphs to explain them. Chris must show the project to her geography teacher at school but also wants to work on it at home. Discuss local and online storage methods that Chris could use and make a recommendation to her.

1.6   Communication networks and entertainment

A network is a group of computers connected together. The Internet is sometimes called a network of networks. It connects computers all over the world mostly using the World Wide Web (www).

The development of broadband means that people have high-speed Internet access at a fairly low cost. It allows businesses, friends and family members to communicate using e-mail and instant messaging.

Businesses advertise their services and sell their products via e-commerce websites. For many businesses, this means they can reach a wider range of customers. Even a small business can sell its goods internationally.

The Internet provides ways for people to entertain themselves by playing games or downloading music and videos. The Internet has become a major source of information. For example, people can do research for school or university or trace their family tree for fun.

The Internet also has disadvantages. Connecting your computer to lots of others increases the chance of damage to your data resulting from a virus. Not all communication is positive. Terrorists, criminals and paedophiles use the Internet to communicate too.

Local Area Networks and Wide Area Networks

A Local Area Network (LAN) connects computers that are fairly close together, usually in the same building. LANs connect computers either via cables or wireless technology. A Wide Area Network (WAN) connects computers that are farther apart. It uses telephone and cable networks or satellites to transmit the data. Large national and international companies are likely to set up WANs for secure transmission of their data.

Communication devices and media

Telephones and VoIP/Internet telephone

There are two main types of telephone: land lines and mobile phones. Mobile phones are extremely convenient, but it costs more to make calls on a mobile phone than using a land line. Mobile phones can also be used to send SMS (text) messages. These messages are cheaper than phone calls and it is now possible to send pictures or even video messages.

A new type of telephone has been developed fairly recently. It uses VoIP (Voice over Internet Protocol). These phones use a broadband connection to transmit voice messages to other users over the Internet. Skype is one example of this. These calls are essentially free, as it is included in the cost of your broadband connection. Some mobile-phone companies are now offering free Skype-to-Skype calls.

E-mail and fax

E-mail is used for communication between businesses and individuals. You type in your message and send it to the other person's e-mail address. The message is sent to their e-mail server, where it waits until they download it. E-mails arrive quickly and are cheap to send. E-mail, chat rooms, forums and bulletin boards are dealt with in more detail in Chapter 5.

Key terms

World Wide Web (www): a system of Internet servers that support a collection of web pages on the Internet which hyperlink to each other.

Local Area Network (LAN): a network connecting computers in the same area/room/building.

Wide Area Network (WAN): a network that covers a geographical area larger than a single building; it may be national or global.

SMS: short message service; a system for sending text messages on mobile phones.

Did you know ??????

A home network (which may be wireless) is both a LAN (local to the area of the house) and also a WAN (sending and receiving information over a wide area).

Fax machines have been used less since e-mail has become popular, but they are still used by some businesses. They work by scanning a paper-based document and sending that image to the other fax machine over the telephone lines. The advantage with faxes is that neither user needs a computer, just a fax machine and a telephone line.

Network devices

Internet connections

Until quite recently most people accessed the Internet using a **modem** connected to a standard telephone line. These dial-up connections used normal telephone lines. They needed a modem to convert **digital signals** to **analog signals** that could be transmitted over the telephone lines. These connections tied up the phone line, so you could not make telephone calls when connected to the Internet.

In most areas of the UK, telephone exchanges have been adapted to deliver broadband connections. These are much faster and do not stop you using the phone at the same time. Most broadband contracts allow you to stay connected for as long as you want for a fixed price. They will usually have a limit on how much data you can download.

Wi-Fi and Bluetooth are both wireless technologies based on radio waves. Bluetooth is used mainly to replace cables as a way of connecting two devices that are close together. You might use Bluetooth to send an image from your phone to your computer. Wi-Fi is used to connect devices to communications networks. An example would be using your laptop in an Internet cafe or on a wireless network at home.

Internet connection speeds control how quickly you can download or upload data. They are measured in megabytes per second. **Bandwidth** measures the capacity of a communications channel. Broadband services have a much higher capacity than narrow band, giving faster data transfer rates. If you want access to your home phone, TV broadband, computer Internet services and music and video streaming at the same time, you need a large amount of bandwidth.

Another way of connecting to the Internet is to use a mobile broadband connection. This involves using a wireless **dongle** that contains a **SIM card**. The dongle acts as a modem to connect the computer to the Internet. The dongles will work wherever there is a suitable 3G signal.

Servers

Servers are used to manage computer networks. There are various types of server. File servers manage the files that you can save on a school network. Printer servers manage printers and the print jobs sent to them. Web servers store the files that make up web pages and they allow you to view them on your computer. E-mail servers store e-mail messages for distribution to users and forward them when requested.

Entertainment systems

TV (terrestrial, digital, cable, broadband) and radio

Until a few years ago the only way of watching TV programmes was through a TV connected to an aerial. This is known as terrestrial TV.

U *A dongle acts as a modem to connect a computer to the Internet*

Many cable companies then started to offer TV services delivered through a network of underground cables. Over the next few years all of the TV programmes offered in the UK will be digital. Many users already watch TV through a digital service, using a set-top box or a digital TV. It is also possible to watch TV or listen to radio programmes on your computer using a broadband service.

Home entertainment

Because TV programmes are delivered digitally, they can be stored on hard drives just like any other computer data. This means that you can record TV programmes to watch later. Digital TV also allows live TV to be paused and restarted later. People can now have **integrated entertainment systems** linking TV, video and music on a range of devices across the home. Games can be played on a TV screen because that data is digital too. TV has also become interactive through digital services. Viewers can take part in quizzes or vote in online programmes.

Music and film downloads

Instead of buying music on CD or films on DVD, many people now download content from websites. MP3 players are small and make it easy to carry around a lot of music and videos. The legal issues surrounding downloads are dealt with in detail in Chapter 7.

> ### Remember
> When talking about a TV programme, the word 'programme' ends 'mme', but a computer 'program' only has one 'm'.

> ### Key terms
> **Integrated entertainment systems:** systems that combine a range of devices offering visual, musical, video, audio and gaming entertainment.

V   *Virgin on Demand service*

Summary questions

1. What equipment do you need to be able to view digital TV?

2. Describe two different ways you could connect your laptop to the Internet.

3. When viewing a programme, what are the advantages of digital TV?

4. Why would Amy buy a music download rather than a CD?

5. New TVs use digital technology. Explain how this can be useful in terms of an integrated entertainment system.

In this chapter you will have learnt:

- ✔ the difference between hardware and software
- ✔ the main hardware components that make up a computer system
- ✔ about the operating system
- ✔ using computer systems and seeking help
- ✔ the features of a variety of input and output devices
- ✔ the units of computer memory and the types of memory available
- ✔ the uses of communication networks and entertainment systems.

> ### Boost your grade!
>
> **Cookies**
>
> Cookies are used to track your website activity, allowing the website to 'remember' you. It can then target the advertisements you see, based on what you have looked at so far. The website stores a small text file on your computer that gives it information about your activity. If you go back to the website your browser sends the cookies back to the server. The hyperlinks you have already followed will be in the 'clicked' rather than 'unclicked' colour. Many companies use cookies to track online transactions (what you have bought).

AQA Examination-style questions

Answer **all** questions in the spaces provided.

1 Which **one** of the following is **not** an input device?

A	Keyboard	B	Scanner
C	Hard disk drive	D	Joystick

(1 mark)

2 Which **one** of the following is **not** an output device?

A	Screen (VDU)	B	Plotter
C	Laser printer	D	Microphone

(1 mark)

3 Which **one** of the following is **not** a storage device?

A	Touch sensitive screen	B	Floppy disk drive
C	CD-ROM drive	D	Magnetic tape unit

(1 mark)

4 Which **one** of the following loses its contents when the computer is switched off?

A	ROM	B	RAM
C	Hard disk	D	Floppy disk

(1 mark)

AQA, June 2007

5 Modern computer systems make use of a variety of methods of data capture, some of which are shown below.

A	bar-codes	B	data logging	C	feedback
D	magnetic strips	E	MICR	F	OCR
G	OMR	H	questionnaires	I	sensor

From the list given above, choose the **most suitable** method of data capture for each of the applications given below.

(a) Used to input students' answers to multiple-choice examination questions. Students put a mark in the box next to their chosen answer. *(1 mark)*

(b) Used to collect information from parents about planned changes to length of the school day. *(1 mark)*

(c) Used to input information from groceries at the supermarket checkout. *(1 mark)*

(d) Used to input information from a credit card when paying for petrol at a garage. *(1 mark)*

(e) Used by banks to input cheque details including the value of the cheque. *(1 mark)*

AQA, June 2008

6 Below is a list of problems that people come across when using ICT.

A	Paper jam	B	Storage full
C	Software freeze	D	Uninstalling software
E	Shortcut not working		

Which problem is being described?

(a) The output on the computer's screen does not respond to input from the keyboard or mouse and the display remains unchanged.

(b) An error that occurs when attempting to save a 2 gigabyte video file on to a CD that can store 900 megabytes. *(2 marks)*

7 Describe **four** tasks that are carried out by an operating system. *(4 marks)*

AQA, June 2006

8 Daniel Chan has just started a new job as a reporter on a local newspaper. He has to choose a password to use on the newspaper's WAN.

(a) What do the letters WAN stand for? *(1 mark)*

(b) Why would it be essential for the newspaper to be connected to a WAN? *(1 mark)*

AQA, June 2008

9 An estate agent, who sells and rents houses, is about to install a new computer system.

(a) Which **two** of the following would be the **most useful** input devices for the company?

A	A monitor	B	A mouse	C	A scanner
D	A modem	E	A joystick	F	An OMR reader

(2 marks)

(b) Which **two** of the following would be the **most useful** output devices for the company?

A	A monitor	B	A dot-matrix printer	C	A scanner
D	A colour laser printer	E	A joystick	F	A CD-ROM drive

(2 marks)

(c) The estate agent is going to install a LAN. What does the abbreviation LAN stand for? *(1 mark)*

(d) Which **two** of the following are advantages to the estate agent of working on a LAN rather than stand-alone machines?

A Reduces expensive telephone calls

B Reduces costs as users can share peripherals

C Allows access to the Internet

D Users can share centrally stored files with details of houses

E The estate agent will be able to work at weekends

(2 marks)

AQA, June 2006

10 **(a)** Which **one** of the following best describes a smart phone?

A An electronic handheld device for playing games only

B An electronic handheld device that integrates a mobile phone with a personal digital assistant and web access

C An electronic handheld device which has a smarter appearance than a standard mobile phone

D An electronic handheld device that operates a television. *(1 mark)*

(b) (i) Describe two advantages of using a smart phone compared with a landline phone (traditional 'home' phone). *(2 marks)*

(ii) Describe two disadvantages of using a smart phone compared with a landline phone (traditional 'home' phone). *(2 marks)*

11 Most personal computers contain a video card. Describe two activities where it is essential that the computer has a high-quality video card. *(4 marks)*

12 You will be marked on your ability to use good English, to organise information clearly and to use specialist vocabulary where appropriate.

A home owner is going to buy a new entertainment system. She is considering buying a terrestrial TV with surround sound, which is cheaper, or a digital integrated entertainment system, which is more expensive. What are the possible advantages **and** disadvantages of each type of system for the home owner? Explain your answer with reference to usability and entertainment issues. *(8 marks)*

2.1   Feasibility studies

One of the main purposes of any ICT system is to solve problems. When a new ICT system is being developed, it follows a path called the systems life cycle. The life cycle has eight main stages. The system is a cycle rather than a straight path because at some point a new system will be needed and the procedure is followed again.

Most organisations use ICT systems to assist with work. They might use them to keep track of their finances, produce a product, manage their stock – it all depends on what the organisation does. From time to time they will introduce a new system. This might be to update the one they already have, or it may be something completely new. When a business or organisation is considering a new ICT system, the first thing they will do is carry out a **feasibility study**.

If something is feasible, it means that it is possible to do. It does not necessarily mean that it will succeed, but the chances are that it will be worth going ahead with. A feasibility study is a process that is carried out to decide whether a project is worth starting or continuing.

▇ Gathering information

The first part of a feasibility study is to find out why the organisation wants a new system. It may be because it might help them to solve a problem or perhaps meet some need that the organisation has. For example:

- A business may have become very successful and need an updated computer system that can cope with the larger number of orders.
- A school might decide it would like to be able to keep better track of the progress of its students.
- A jeweller working at home might decide that selling their products through a website may attract more customers.

What information is needed?

Remember that the purpose of a feasibility study is to decide whether to proceed with the project. There will be time for more detailed analysis later, but for the moment the important information is as follows:

- **Who** is the **client**? Is the system going to be for an individual, a business or some other organisation? A little bit of background information is useful.
- **What** is the problem? What does the client want the new system to do?
- **How** is the problem currently handled? There may be a manual system in place, or perhaps a computer system that is no longer

good enough. If the problem is a new one, there may be no current system at all.

- **Who** will use the system? The client may have decided that the system is needed, but they may not be the **user** of it. Will their staff use it? Will they manage ICT support within the organisation?

- **What** resources are available? This might include existing hardware and software, but people are also important. Their skills are an important resource. If the users' skills need to be improved, then training will need to be arranged to suit their needs.

- **What** is the time scale? When does the new system have to be working?

Techniques used to gather information

Interviews

The most obvious way of finding out what a client needs is to ask them. It is difficult to imagine developing any system without talking to the person who needs it. Interviews are very useful because they allow discussion. One person can ask a question, the other person gives their answer, and they can both talk about anything that is unclear. Face-to-face contact allows you to see the other person's facial expressions and body language. They also help to build trust. Interviews can take up a lot of time, and it is easy to wander off the main topic, so it is important to prepare in advance.

If the project goes ahead, much more detailed follow-up interviews will be needed as part of the analysis of the system.

Questionnaires

A questionnaire can be given to lots of people at once. This is a quicker way of gathering the information than carrying out lots of interviews. Questionnaires tend to be cheap to produce and administer. They can be answered anonymously (without revealing the identities of the people who answered them) and completed at a convenient time.

A well-designed questionnaire may also be easier to analyse on computer than the results of an interview. This is because the responses that can be given are much more limited, especially if **closed questions** are used.

An **open question** allows the person filling in the questionnaire to write anything at all. A closed question limits the responses they can make. Not everyone likes filling in questionnaires and some may deliberately include silly answers.

A *Face-to-face interview*

Open question: How often do you use the Internet?

Responses could be any of the following or something else: 'quite a lot', 'not much', 'every evening', 'when I feel like it', 'only when I need to'.

All of those responses are valid, but they do not make it very easy to analyse the results.

Closed question: Do you use the Internet:

a Every day?

b Three or more days a week?

c Fewer than three days a week?

d Never?

The closed question gives a much clearer picture of how often the sample of people surveyed use the Internet. The answers can be gathered and easily analysed.

The number of people that the questionnaire is given to is known as the **sample size**. The bigger the sample size the more reliable the results should be. However, a bigger sample will cost more and take longer to collect and analyse.

A paper-based questionnaire is quite simple to produce, but all of the results have to be entered onto the computer manually. The same questionnaire filled in online can be linked to a database so that the responses are captured automatically. This speeds up the process and may reduce errors. If the questionnaire only includes closed questions, OMR (optical mark recognition, for example an answer sheet for a multiple-choice exam) forms might be a suitable method of collecting the data. This type does need specialised forms and software.

OCR (optical character recognition, for example a passport application form) forms are also a possibility, with the responses written letter by letter into squares drawn on the form. Again, specialist equipment is required. OMR and OCR should be considered if there are a lot of responses to analyse.

Observation

It can be extremely useful to watch an existing system working. You can sometimes notice things that the people using the system are not aware of. Observation allows you to make your own decisions about what is happening in the system.

Your results are not likely to be affected by biased answers from users. If a system is used for a long time, people get used to it and take certain things for granted. Someone else watching that system may spot things that slow it down. Observation does not interfere with the running of the business and you may notice things that have not been thought about or discussed in an interview or questionnaire.

Feasibility report

At the end of a feasibility study you will need to write a report to sum up what you have found out. This would need to cover the following points:

- if the system is likely to be feasible in technical terms, whether a system can be made that will solve the problem
- the most likely way of producing the solution
- whether the cost of the system fits into the budget available
- whether it is possible to get the system finished in time to meet the deadline
- how the developers will judge whether the final solution is successful.

The stages of the systems life cycle

Feasibility study

A feasibility study is the first stage in developing a new system. Once a new system has been produced, it is not really finished. The system will need to be maintained as things around it change, and eventually the decision may be taken to replace it. At that point, the cycle starts again.

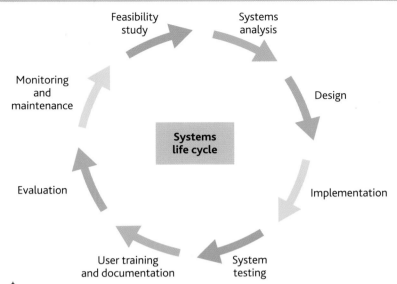

B *The systems life cycle is a continuous process*

Systems analysis

A feasibility study involves analysing the current situation, but systems analysis does it in more detail. The aim is to state exactly what the new system needs to achieve. It will need to examine:

- What data needs to be input, its format and the quantity of data. For example, are there likely to be five transactions each day or 500?
- What information needs to be produced and in what format?
- What processing will be needed to turn that input into the correct output?
- What hardware and software are currently available?
- Who will the users be and what are their skill levels and training needs?
- What performance criteria will be used to judge the final solution?

Design

The first phase of the cycle defined what the new system needs to do. The design phase deals with how the system is going to do it. It also specifies how the system will be constructed. It is during this phase that plans are drawn up regarding how the system will be tested.

Plans for construction

Time planning

First it is necessary to write down a list of tasks that need to been done as the system is being built. The next job is to set a time to complete each of those tasks so that the overall system is finished in time to meet the deadlines (these are sometimes called milestones).

System design

The exact design tasks that will need to be completed will obviously depend on the system that is being produced. However, in any system it will be necessary to consider how it will work and what the user interface will be.

Functional design

At this stage it is necessary to decide what software will be best for building the system. Sometimes that will mean choosing between two different types of package, for example a spreadsheet or a database. Sometimes it might mean choosing between two similar packages, for example two different web authoring packages with different features.

Once the package has been selected, a decision has to be made about how to use the functions it provides to make a system that works efficiently. The content, its layout and how it will be formatted are considerations that must all be addressed. Then the designs must be documented in a way that is appropriate for that package, for example:

- **Spreadsheets** – a sheet for each page showing which cells will contain the text, numbers and formulae. It is also necessary to show what the formulae are and what they do. Other features such as validated cells and conditional formatting should be shown too.
- **Websites** – a sheet for each page of the site showing the objects on them and how the sheets are linked. It is also good practice to produce a list of files that will be linked in, for example graphics, videos and text files, and where they will be stored, so that the hyperlinks will work efficiently.

Interface design

Hardware

The user interface controls how the user will interact with the system. It involves the input and output devices they will use as well as the screen layout they will see. Input and output devices should be chosen with both the user and the task in mind. (Input and output devices are covered in more detail in Chapter 1, pages 16–20.)

⚭ **links**

Chapters 3 and 4 (pages 38–53 and 56–68) give you more information about software features that need to be considered in the functional design stage.

> **Example**
>
> A bar-code reader is a useful device. It is easy to use and has built-in validation, which speeds up data entry for the user. However, it is only possible to input numbers, so it is only suitable for applications where long numbers need to be input. A school library is a good example of where a bar-code reader is a useful input device.

C Bar-code reader

Screen layouts

The screen layout needs to be suitable for both the user and the task. An interface with bright colours and bold shapes might be suitable for an educational game for a young child, but it would be very tiring on the eyes of an adult user entering data all day. An interface for a very young child should use little or no text, relying much more on pictures and sounds.

When designing a system that is to be used for long periods at a time, consideration should also be given to the health and safety of the user. The screen colours, fonts and font sizes should be chosen to make the screen easy to read without making the users' eyes too tired. It is necessary to think about the ease of use and the risk of repetitive strain injury. It is best to avoid the user having to scroll around the screen more than is absolutely necessary. Using check boxes and drop-down lists can avoid the user having to type in long pieces of text.

Design sheets

A design sheet should be made for all of the screens in the system. The design sheet should show the sizes and colours of the objects on the screen, with an explanation of what each object does.

Testing plan

There is no point in building an ICT system that does not work or is difficult to use. The only way to be sure that a system does what it needs to do is to test it. It may seem strange to plan the testing this early in a project, but it is important to decide what needs to be tested, when the testing needs to be done, how it will be carried out and what data will be used.

The testing that is required will depend on the software being used:

- Spreadsheet – is all of the data and information displayed correctly, does each formula produce the correct answer, does the validation work as expected?
- Website – are there any spelling mistakes or grammatical errors, do the pictures display correctly, do all of the hyperlinks go to the right place, do the pages load in an acceptable time, do the pages display on a range of browsers and at different resolutions?
- Database – do the searches produce the correct results, does the validation work as expected, do the forms and reports show the correct fields and is all of the information displayed correctly?
- Multimedia presentation – does the presentation load and run correctly, does it contain the correct information, are the text and graphics appropriately sized, are the timings for each section correct, is it suitable for its target audience?

The tests above are all concerned with how the system works, but every system should also be appropriate for its user. This means that the users need to be involved with the testing. They can then give their opinions about changes that might need to be made.

At the end of the design phase there should be:

- a list of all the tasks that must be done and the deadline for each one
- a set of designs that show how the system is to be built
- a testing plan that states the tests that will be carried out, what data will be used for them, and what the expected result of each test should be.

Implementation

Once the designs have been completed, the system needs to be built. This is known as implementation. Implementation should follow the **plan for construction**, and each feature will need to be tested as it is produced, following the **testing plan**.

As a solution is implemented, it may turn out that the designs need to be changed. This may be because the original designs did not work or a better way of doing something has been discovered. That is fine, but the changes should be documented.

At the end of the implementation stage there should be:

- a working system
- details of any changes that were made to the designs.

System testing 🄺

As mentioned above, testing is not something that just happens at the end of a project. It needs to take place as the system is being built, so that mistakes are corrected before the next section is implemented. This is actually a natural way of working. For example, if a formula is written into a spreadsheet cell, it is natural to make sure it works before moving on to the next task.

It is important that a record is kept of the testing that is carried out and the results of it. If changes need to be made as a result of tests that fail, then that needs to be documented too.

User testing also needs to be documented. After all, there is no point in producing a system that the user is not happy with.

User training and documentation

In the analysis stage of the life cycle, the users' skills were established. From this the amount of training that each user needs can be decided. A novice user will require more detail about each step of the process than an experienced one.

Most systems will also need some technical documentation that shows how the system works and what its structure is. For example, spreadsheets should show details of formulae, validation and cell protection. This is because at some point in the future the system may need to be changed, and someone will need to understand its structure. The design sheets may form part of this documentation.

Evaluation

Evaluation is an important stage in the life cycle of a system. It involves looking carefully at the system that has been produced and deciding whether or not it does what it set out to do. At the end of the systems analysis section, a list of **performance criteria** is produced. These will help decide how successful the implementation has been.

An evaluation looks at each of the performance criteria and judges how well the system matches them. If some of the performance criteria were not met, it examines the reasons for that and what can be done so that the system does match the criteria.

What next?

Another question that should be asked at this stage is: 'What next?' This looks at how the system might be developed in the future. This might be to improve the current system or extend it to do more things.

Self-evaluation

At the end of any major task that you carry out, you should always ask yourself how well you think you did it. Identifying your strengths and weaknesses will help you to improve your performance on the next task that you undertake.

It is important to be realistic rather than to grumble about things. For example, it is not appropriate for an evaluation to say, 'I did not complete my testing because my user was too busy to see me'. The truth is more likely to be, 'I did not book an appointment with my user in advance, and so he was not able to test my system in time for my final deadline'. That statement is useful because it identifies that it is important to book appointments.

Monitoring and maintenance

Delivering a new system is not the end of the systems life cycle. The system needs to be monitored. That means keeping a close eye on it to make sure that it continues to perform at an acceptable standard.

Over a period of time, the system may need to be maintained for a variety of reasons, for example:

- errors may be found that were not discovered in the original testing, and these will need to be corrected
- the situation itself may change, for example an invoicing system that adds VAT at 17.5 per cent will need to be changed if the VAT rate changes to 15 per cent
- the user may decide that a new feature needs to be added or an existing one changed.

This maintenance happens all the time with commercial software. Anti-virus software needs to be updated to cope with new viruses that have been produced. Operating systems need to cope with new hardware and software or new security threats. Often these updates are carried out by downloading a **patch** from the company's website. Eventually, the client may decide that the system needs to be completely redesigned or replaced, and so the systems life cycle starts again with a feasibility study.

Information sources

At various stages of the systems life cycle information will be needed. Some of that information will come from people, using interviews or questionnaires. At other times it will be necessary to use other sources, some ICT-based and some not.

These days, there is a tendency to assume that the Internet is always the best place to find information. Websites certainly have lots of information, but they are not always accurate or truthful.

Other web-based sources may include podcasts and blogs, wikis and online databases. Podcasts and blogs may be from professional organisations, such as the BBC, or they may be posted by individuals. Anyone can add facts to a wiki, and there is no guarantee that they will be accurate.

CDs and DVD-ROMs can be a good source of accurate information. These sources of information will have been checked before they were published and they are likely to be accurate. Electronic material may be easier to search than paper-based books. Many books are now also published in an electronic format, known as an e-book. If you need information that is absolutely up to date, these sources may not be as suitable as websites and newspapers that are updated more frequently.

Magazines and newspapers can be useful sources of information. Specialist magazines are available on many topics and they often contain good comparisons of products. National newspapers may give you national and international information. Local newspapers can be an excellent way of finding out about suppliers in your neighbourhood and events that are happening close to where you live.

links

Podcasts, blogs, wikis and online databases are covered in more detail in Chapter 5.

links

www.upmystreet.com is an online database that allows you to search for information about any area based on its postcode. You can find out information about the area itself, such as crime rates and property prices. You can also look for suppliers of goods and services.

Finding good-quality information

In order to check the quality of your information:

- Check the information you find with another source. This will help you to check that it is accurate and not biased.
- Look at the url (web address) of any websites you use to help you to find out who created the information.
- Check the publication date. In some cases, especially when looking for information about new technology, you need to make sure the information is up to date.

Summary questions

1 A shopping centre would like an interactive information system to help shoppers find their way around. You have been asked to carry out a feasibility study to help them decide whether or not to go ahead. Give one example of where you would use:

a interviews

b questionnaires

c observation.

2 You are designing the interactive system for the shopping centre using a touch screen for input and output.

a What features of a touch screen make it suitable for use in a shopping centre?

b What tests would you need to carry out on such a system? Give reasons for your answers.

3 Once the shopping centre system is up and running, it might need maintenance. Give two situations where maintenance might be needed.

4 An online shopping site has a form that customers fill in to place an order. The designer has been told to use validation wherever possible.

a Explain what validation means and why the designer has been asked to use it.

b Give three fields that could be validated and describe a different type of validation used for each one.

5 A complex spreadsheet is used to keep track of sales forecasts in a large company. Describe two types of user documentation that might be needed for different users of this system.

In this chapter you will have learnt:

✔ that ICT systems development follows the systems life cycle

✔ that a feasibility study is carried out before proceeding with the project

✔ that systems analysis defines what the system needs to do

✔ what needs to be included when designing a system and a testing plan

✔ that implementation means building the system

✔ that a new system needs to be tested thoroughly to check that it works and the client is happy with it

✔ that users need documentation that suits their skill level

✔ that analysis helps you to build a better system next time

✔ that systems need to be monitored and maintained

✔ how to find good-quality information.

AQA Examination-style questions

1 The stages in the development of a new computer system include Analysis, Design, Implementation, Testing and Evaluation. Below are some of the tasks that usually take place during the production of a new computer system.

A Considering how well the new system works
B Deciding the features of the software needed
C Entering test data
D Finding out how the present system works
E Planning screen and report layouts
F Preparing a test plan
G Setting up a suitable database
H Setting up performance criteria and desired outcomes
I Suggesting future improvements to the new system

For each of the questions below, write the letter or letters for the answers.
(a) Which **two** of these would take place during the Analysis stage? *(2 marks)*
(b) Give **three** of these that would take place during the Design stage. *(3 marks)*
(c) Which **one** of these would take place during the Testing stage? *(1 mark)*
(d) Give **one** of these that would take place during the Evaluation stage. *(1 mark)*

AQA, June 2008

2 Which **one** of the following would be **most** useful for finding information to write an article about the Prime Minister?
A a web log
B an online database
C a text message
D an Internet search engine *(1 mark)*

3 How does verification help to ensure the accuracy of data? *(2 marks)*

4 A travel company is going to install a computer system for the staff to book holidays online. They need to design a user interface for the holiday booking system.
(a) Which **one** of the following is a type of user interface that could be used for the new system?
A Sensor driven B Link driven C Menu driven *(1 mark)*

(b) Which **one** of these factors should be taken into consideration when designing the new user interface?
A Consistency of layout B Cheap holidays C The need to take regular breaks *(1 mark)*

(c) Give **two** other factors that should be taken into consideration when designing the new user interface. *(2 marks)*

AQA, June 2007

5 A college has just developed a new computer program for processing examination results. The system needs to be tested using a test plan.
(a) At which stage of the systems life cycle would the test plan be produced? *(1 mark)*
(b) Which **two** of the following would you expect to find in the test plans?
A A printout of the computer program
B A list of all tests to be carried out
C An annotated design of the program
D Changes to be made as a result of testing
E Expected results *(2 marks)*
(c) Give **two** reasons why a test plan is needed. *(2 marks)*

AQA, June 2008

3.1 Applications software 🔵k!

It is possible for you to write a letter, produce a professional-looking poster, design an animated presentation and create a website all whilst sitting at your computer. The software that enables you to do this is called applications software.

Each type of applications software is designed to enable you to carry out a specific type of task. In this chapter you will learn the main features of each type of software, what sort of tasks can be accomplished using the software, and how to select the most appropriate software for a given situation.

Applications software is designed to carry out user-related tasks to solve problems. The software is **task specific**. You will have used a number of different types of application software already. Table **A** lists all of the types of applications software along with examples of each.

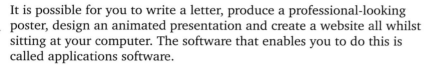

A *Protein values of different foods*

Applications software type	Examples of applications software
Word processors	Microsoft Word, OpenOffice Writer
Desktop publishing software	Microsoft Publisher, Adobe InDesign, Serif Pageplus
Presentation software	Microsoft PowerPoint, OpenOffice Impress, StarImpress, GoogleDocs Presentation
Graphics software	Photoshop, GIMP, Imagine!, Ultimate Paint
Web-design software	Adobe Dreamweaver, Serif Webplus

Other examples of applications software include everything from graphics manipulation software to spreadsheets, databases and web browsing. You will learn more about these types of applications software in the next few chapters.

▮ Generic features of applications software

You can do lots of tasks using software. You might want to produce a music track or create a newsletter. These tasks might seem very different, but the software used has some common features. For example, you might want to copy and paste a sound file, or copy and paste a name. These sorts of features are called **generic features**.

Here are some generic features and a brief description of each:

- **Help** – this provides assistance on how to use the applications software. The help library can be installed on your computer and it is also online.

- **Edit text size** – size is usually measured in points. Paragraph text is typically between 8 and 12 points.
- **Copy** – this copies the current selection to the clipboard.
- **Cut** – this copies the current selection to the clipboard then deletes the selection.
- **Paste** – this inserts the contents of the clipboard.

There are many more generic features in applications software. For a full list of these see the Appendix on pages 131–136.

Open source and proprietary software

Open source means that the software code is freely available (at no cost) for people to use, copy and edit. An example of open source software would be the Linux operating system. Linux is free to download and use, and software developers can also view and edit the code.

Proprietary software is software that you pay to use, but you are not given access to the coding behind it and are not permitted to edit or change the code. An example of proprietary software would be Microsoft Windows. People pay to use Windows, and the coding behind it remains secret.

Advantages of open source software

- The software is free. Proprietary software can be expensive.
- The software code can be developed by a community of developers in a collaborative way. This results in rapid addition of new features and fast fixing of any bugs.
- It can be customised for specific applications.

Advantages of proprietary software

- The developers of proprietary software usually provide a good service, and good follow-up or customer support.
- The software usually comes with automatic updates – this is not always the case with open source software.
- The company is responsible for the integrity and legality of the code it is selling. It must ensure that the code is robust and won't cause harm to a computer system.

Hosted and locally installed applications

Historically, all applications were installed locally on your computer. More recently, with widespread access to fast Internet connections, some software is run on central servers and accessed online. These are called hosted or web-based applications. Common examples of web-based applications are Hotmail and Google Docs. Common examples of locally installed applications would be Microsoft Windows or Open Office.

Activity 3.1

Generic features in two different applications

- Open a word-processing package like Microsoft Word.
- Choose five generic features from the task bar. Using the Help feature, find out how to use each of your chosen features.
- Create a table containing each of the five features and a short description of each.

Now repeat these steps, this time using different applications software such as StarImpress, Adobe Photoshop Elements or Microsoft Excel. Note that not every single generic feature is found in **all** applications. A generic feature appears in **most** applications, but there are exceptions.

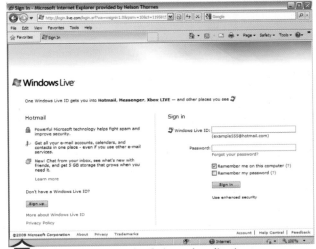

B *Hotmail is an example of a hosted application*

Advantages of hosted applications

- Low start-up costs. Some hosted applications are free to use; those that are aren't free often charge a monthly subscription fee instead of an up-front payment.
- You don't need to install software upgrades – this is managed centrally.
- Since data is stored online, backup is handled automatically by the software developer
- You can access the application and the data from anywhere in the world – and from any PC that has access to the Internet.

Disadvantages of hosted applications

- User needs to be online to use the software.
- If the internet connection is slow, the application runs slowly.
- There are some concerns over security and lack of control over stored data.

Advantages of locally installed applications

- User has more control, since data and software are stored locally.
- They are not reliant on an Internet connection – full functionality of software is available when offline.

Disadvantages of locally installed applications

- They typically involve a large one-off cost.
- Users have to download regular software updates.
- They can use up a lot of computer memory.

Summary questions

1 Look at the document below. List the nine generic features that you can see have been used to create the page.

> Healthy eating: Handout A
>
> # Packing a healthy lunch!
>
> **Lunchbox angels**
> Brown bread
> Fruit
> Water
> Fruit juice
> Low fat yoghurt
> Nuts
>
> **Lunchbox devils**
> Cakes
> Chocolate bars
> Biscuits
> Fizzy drinks
> Crisps
> Sweets
>
> *Healthy swaps...*
>
> White bread Brown bread
> Chocolate bar ➡ Muesli bar
> Dessert pot ➡ Low fat yoghurt
> Fizzy drink ➡ Fruit juice
> Sweets ➡ Nuts
> Crisps ➡ Fruit
>
> 1

2 Give one example of when you might use each of the following features:

a Print Screen

b Find and Replace

c Templates.

3 Which feature is most appropriate for each of the following tasks?

a Omar has a six-page Word document. The content is finished but the layout needs some work. He would like to view all six pages on the screen at once. What tool would you recommend?

b Tatyana has a wide panoramic photo that she wants to insert in a document with some text underneath. At the moment the page is too narrow for the image to fit properly on the page, and the lower half of the page is empty. What would you recommend?

c Luca has a 20-page document that he is about to submit as coursework. Before submitting it he needs to add his name and page numbers to every page. Which feature would help him to do this quickly?

3.2 Word processing and desktop publishing

You will almost certainly have used a **word processor** before, but you may not have used **desktop publishing** software. A simple definition of desktop publishing software is: software that combines graphics and word-processing tools to allow the user to create professional-looking printed documents.

Word-processing software is quite similar to desktop publishing software in many ways. If you have used both types of software you will already know that many of the features can be found in both, for example:

- edit text
- columns
- spelling and grammar checker.

There are many more common features. For a more complete list take a look at the Appendix on pages 131–136.

Designers of word-processing software are continually adding new features, many of which used to be found only in desktop publishing software. The designers of desktop publishing software are also adding word-processing features. This has resulted in fewer differences between the two types of software. However, there are still some clear rules about which software to use. You need to know that:

- Word processors deal with text documents, for example letters and essays.
- Desktop publishers deal with text and graphic publications, for example posters and leaflets.

Word processing or desktop publishing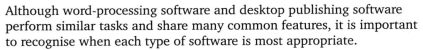

Although word-processing software and desktop publishing software perform similar tasks and share many common features, it is important to recognise when each type of software is most appropriate.

The main difference becomes apparent when you want to create a professional-looking, well laid-out document that contains images. To help you understand how to choose the most appropriate software we will look at two different scenarios:

1 Zach needs to produce a one-page document listing current committee members, a photo of each and some contact details. He will print out 10 to place on various school notice boards.

2 ABProp is a large public company. It needs a 10-page document showing a photo and short background of each board member. It will be enclosed with the annual report and sent out to over 10,000 shareholders.

Essentially, both of these situations need a very similar-looking document, but they would not necessarily be created using the same applications software.

Look at the solution to each scenario on page 42 to help understand how to select the most appropriate software.

> **Key terms**
>
> **Word processor:** a type of applications software used to create text documents.
>
> **Desktop publishing:** also known as DTP. A type of applications software used to create printed materials containing text and images.

> **Did you know** ??????
>
> There are many examples of errors appearing in newspapers as a result of automatically spell-checking an article without looking at it. One example was an article in the *Denver Post* that turned the Harry Potter villain Voldemort into Voltmeter!

Scenario 1: a word processor would be the most suitable choice because:

- it does not matter if the document does not look professional – it is only for school notice boards
- images need to be placed on the page, but it will be a simple layout and there is only one page.

Scenario 2: a desktop publisher would be the most suitable choice because:

- a DTP will make it easier to create a professional-looking cover than a word processor
- images and logos can be more accurately positioned for a smarter appearance
- within the 10 pages there will be a large number of photographs to organise. These will be much easier to position using a DTP package than a word processor.

The choice of whether to use a word processor or desktop publisher is often a question of which one will do the job best, or which will be easiest to use. You will find that for many situations you could actually do the job using either – so you need to analyse which would be the most appropriate.

Case study

What features of desktop publishing do companies use in industry?

This book was created using a combination of word-processing software and desktop publishing software.

The authors wrote the material in a word processor using style templates. The content was finalised and checked for errors using features such as word count and spelling and grammar check.

The styled Word documents were then imported into a desktop publishing package. The DTP software recognised the styles created in the Word documents. That meant minimal reformatting, which reduced errors and saved a lot of time.

A DTP package was also used to create the cover. Features such as transparency, colour gradients, drop shadows and text effects allowed the designers to experiment with a variety of different effects.

Activity 3.2

Analyse the requirements

- Discuss and write a list of the main similarities between the scenarios of Zach and ABProp.
- Discuss and write a list of the main differences in the requirements of Zach and ABProp.

AQA *Examiner's tip*

Whilst many documents can be created using either a word processor or a desktop publisher, in the exam you should remember that text-only documents are best handled by a word processor, and documents containing both text and images are best created using a DTP package.

links

www.quark.com/en (Quark) and www.adobe.com/products/indesign/customers (Adobe InDesign). These are the two most commonly used desktop publishing packages.

Summary questions

Look at this document about Saint Felix Open Day.

Saint Felix Open Day: 22nd April

Saint Felix would like to to welcome all potential students and parents to an upcoming Open Day. The day will include a tour all the facilities, and provide an opportunity to meet the headmistress and speak with teachers of all subjects.

Timetable Of the day:

10am: Coffee and registration Reception

10.30am: Introduction to Saint Felix by Mrs. Campbell, Headmistress   Assembly Hall

11am: Tour of the new Performing Arts facilities   Meet at Performing Arts block

12pm: Lunch   Canteen

1pm: Tour of the sports facilities   Gym

2pm: Exhibition of students' work   DT & Art Department

3pm: Overview of extracurricular activitaes (see below).

4–6pm: Open question and answer sessions with teachers, see table overleaf for details of subject teachers & locations

Extracurricular activities

Saint Felix also has a wide variety of extra curricular activities that pupils can get involved with. These include:
Duke of Edinburgh's Award
Chess Club
School trip such as skiing
Optional subject field trips
Squash league
Language exchange programmes

Open question and answer session details

Subject	Teacher(s)			Location
Maths	Mr. Ratcliff	Mrs. Warne	Mrs. Gosling	Assembly Hall
English	Mrs. Roberts	Mrs. Holland		English Block
History	Mr. Iqbal			Humanities Block
Geography	Miss. Chang			Assembly Hall
DT & Art	Mr. Kite			DT & Art Block
Performing Arts	Mrs. Leicester			Performing Arts Block
Science	Mrs. Alka			Assembly Hall
Sport	Miss. Maskell			Assembly Hall
Languages	Mrs. College	Mr. Dixon		Assembly Hall

Map of Saint Felix School

1. List three errors in the document.

2. Suggest how the following features could be used to improve the layout of the document:
   a. text fonts and styles
   b. tables
   c. bullets
   d. section breaks
   e. page orientation
   f. layering (order of images on the page)
   g. merge/split table cells.

3. For each of the following documents and tasks, state whether a word processor or a desktop publisher would be most appropriate:
   a. writing a simple curriculum vitae (CV)
   b. designing a poster to advertise a school play
   c. writing an essay for history coursework
   d. creating a multi-page booklet on paintings done by school pupils, along with text about each artist, for a charity artwork auction.

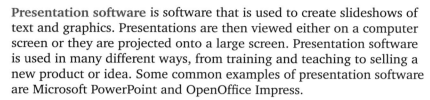

3.3 Presentation software 🅚

Presentation software is software that is used to create slideshows of text and graphics. Presentations are then viewed either on a computer screen or they are projected onto a large screen. Presentation software is used in many different ways, from training and teaching to selling a new product or idea. Some common examples of presentation software are Microsoft PowerPoint and OpenOffice Impress.

Take a look at the three situations below which show different examples of when presentation software might be used:

- Kamal has created a **multimedia** presentation about the Duke of Edinburgh's award expedition. It contains photos, a short video and bulleted lists. He uses this to help with his talk about his expedition.

- A school has an electronic bulletin board in their reception. They have a short presentation informing visitors about things that are happening in the school that week. The slides automatically change every few seconds, showing text, graphics and photos.

- An advertising salesman for a magazine has created a short **interactive presentation** that lists some magazine statistics mixed in with many attention-grabbing images of the publication. He e-mails this as an attachment to potential customers who enquire about advertising in the magazine.

Each of these presentations will use different features. There are a variety of features common to all presentation software that you need to be familiar with:

- Insert slide – add a new slide to a new presentation.
- Enter and edit text – enter slide titles and content, edit text fonts and sizes.
- Insert pictures – add photos, diagrams, images, etc. to a slide.
- Insert buttons – add buttons to slides that perform actions such as 'Go to slide 3' or play a sound.
- Create hyperlinks – make hyperlinks on a slide that link to other slides, or to a document on your computer, or to a page on the Internet.

For a full list of presentation software features see the Appendix on pages 131–136.

C *Presentation software can be used to sell a new product or idea*

Activity 3.3

Use a search engine to find an online presentation that you can download. Try searching for 'online prospectus.ppt' – look for search results containing PowerPoint .ppt files. Download the presentations and look at which features have been used.

Activity 3.4

Create a short presentation

Imagine you are on holiday and a representative of a local scuba diving club is coming to do a presentation at your hotel about scuba diving courses. He has written the text for each slide and he has some underwater photos to add. He has asked you if you can make the presentation a bit more interesting.

- Create a four-page presentation with the following text on each page.
- Use Google to download some underwater photos (search Google Images for 'anemone fish', 'blue spotted stingray' and 'seahorse').
- Add some colour and background, resize the images and change the font styles to make the presentation look a bit more interesting. Add a fish logo to every page using the page template (also called a Slide Master).
- Experiment with various animation, transition and sound effects.
- Play the slideshow to test out the new effects.
- You can make the presentation more interactive by adding hyperlinks and buttons. Think about how you might use those features then add one of each (you can insert additional slides if you like).

> **Learn to Scuba Dive!**
>
> Become an Open Water Diver
> with Cristal Dive, Koh Tao, Thailand

Slide 1

> **Course Timetable**
>
> 3 Day course
> Day 1:
> - Learn some scuba diving theory before getting in the water
> Day 2:
> - Practise using scuba equipment in a swimming pool

Slide 2

> **Course Timetable**
>
> Day 3:
> - 2 open water dives at one of the following locations
>   – Twin Peaks
>   – Mango Bay
>   – White Rock
> Dive site location will depend on dive boat schedule.

Slide 3

> **Dive site location: Twin Peaks**
>
> - What is there to see?
> - Koh Toa dive site map

Slide 4

Summary questions

1 For the three presentations mentioned on page 44 think of three specific features that the presentation software would need to have in order to create each presentation.

2 Write a short description of how you would use each of the following features:
a print screen
b hyperlinks
c slide handouts
d buttons
e animation
f sound effects
g template/master slide.

3 Zebra Designs is a design agency based in London. It works for a variety of clients across the UK. It has a large portfolio of work that it has done for clients, from simple flyers to websites and online presentations. Make a list of three features of applications software that you think they would find most useful. Give a reason why they would find each feature useful in multimedia design.

Graphics production and image manipulation software is used to create and draw images as well as to edit existing images and photos. There are many reasons why graphics software is used both at home and in industry. Here are some examples of how graphics software is used:

- cropping a photo or changing it to black and white instead of colour
- changing the image size of a drawing to reduce the file size so that it can be e-mailed
- cleaning up marks that appear on a scanned document
- placing a photo of a model against a library shot of a beach for a travel advert
- airbrushing out a bruise on a model's arm for a magazine cover.

You need to be familiar with a selection of features common to all graphics software. Features such as brush and airbrush tools, shading, text box and layering can be used to create a drawing in a graphics package. There are many additional features that are used in image manipulation packages such as Photoshop. The Appendix on pages 131–136 has a full description of the common features of graphics software.

> **Key terms**
>
> **Filter**: in graphics software, a filter is a process that changes the appearance of an image. Filters are used to create specific effects, for example blur, pixelate and add brush strokes.

Example

Joseph finds a very old family photo whilst helping his mum to clear out the attic. His mum is pleased to find the photo but is upset that it has been damaged – there are some small rips and creases as well as some discolouration on it. Joseph decides to try and clean up the photo and have it framed as a present.

The first thing Joseph does is to scan in the photo. Next he uses a graphics package to:

- rotate the image slightly anticlockwise (because the scan was not completely straight)
- crop the untidy border
- airbrush out small scratches and spots
- remove tiny marks using a dust and scratches **filter** – this is a feature found in Photoshop.

Then he printed the photo on high-gloss photo paper and put it in a frame.

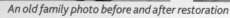
D *An old family photo before and after restoration*

Activity 3.5

Create a picture round for a quiz

Often in a pub quiz night one of the rounds is a picture round. Each of the quiz teams will be given a one-page sheet with 10 images on it. There is one question based on every image.

Use the techniques below to create a one-page sheet for the picture round with 10 questions:

1 'Guess the celebrity' questions: first download some photos of celebrities. Use the following features to distort the photos so that people have to guess who is in each photo:

  a morphing

  b image size – change the size so that the image is stretched

  c paintbrush

  d eraser

  e repeating pattern (cut out a section of the photo and use it to create a repeating pattern).

2 'Guess the headline' questions: scan in some headlines from a magazine. Use a graphics package to crop the headline so there is no other text around it. Now use the paintbrush or eraser tools to blank out one or two words from the headline.

3 'Spot the difference': start with two identical photos and make small changes to one of them, for example you could erase an object.

4 Finally, insert the images into a word-processing document and add the questions (or, for a more professional-looking quiz, use a DTP package). Remember to add question numbers! Print the page and give it to a friend to try.

AQA *Examiner's tip*

You should be familiar with the different types of image that image manipulation software is used for, such as photos, scanned images and drawings.

Summary questions

1 Emma has been asked to produce the graphics for an advert to put in her school newsletter. The advert is for T-shirts with the name and logo of the school football team on them. Emma has two photos of someone wearing the T-shirt, one showing the front and one showing the back. Her brief is to show the T-shirt without the person modelling it, on a red background. List the steps she should take to do this and the tools and features she would use.

2 You want to create a simple drawing of some fireworks for use in an advert for the school fireworks night. Explain how you might use the following tools and features to create the drawing:

  a curved line

  b various brush shapes

  c airbrush tool

  d pick colour.

3.5 Web design ⓚ

Websites are used by individuals and companies to capture the attention of potential clients. The purpose of the website may be to tell visitors about a person, or to explain about a company's products or services. In order to do this a website must be designed so that it is interesting for people to view and they can easily find the information they are looking for. There is a range of applications software that helps to create websites, and there are many advanced features for creating eye-catching effects.

A website is a collection of single web pages that are linked together using hyperlinks. The website structure depends on how these pages are linked. When you first create a website, you sketch out each page and specify which page the hyperlink leads to.

Home page

Evaluation login

Order page

E *Here are a few pages from the* kerboodle! *website*

The website is made up of a collection of web pages, each linked together by hyperlinks. You can find out how a website is organised by looking at where the hyperlinks on each page take you. Look at three of the web pages from the *kerboodle!* website:

- The Home page has feature panels that are updated regularly to reflect current events and new products that Nelson Thornes is trying to promote. The feature panels are designed to grab the user's attention through the use of a variety of images and colours.

- Evaluation login allows users to log in to their accounts. Not all websites have this feature, but most online banks and online shops such as Amazon will require the user to have an account.

- The order page allows customers to place orders online or give contact details for customer services. Notice that in addition to the top menu bar (containing Home, Login, etc.) there are additional hyperlinks within the page for each of the publications being offered. Each hyperlink is linked to a separate page that contains images and descriptions of each product.

Activity 3.6

Website analysis

Choose one of the following websites to analyse, or choose one of your own:

- www.ecurie25.co.uk
- www.crystaldive.com
- http://theraceway.com
- www.asos.com.

For your chosen website:

- On the home page, identify which parts are on the template and which parts are unique to that page.
- Using the print screen feature, paste four of the web pages into one document. Draw lines to represent where the links are between the four pages.

Flash

Flash is applications software that is used to create animation effects for websites, such as a moving icon, short movie or rotating photo. It is possible to create an entire website in Flash. However, Flash is commonly used to create effects that are inserted into websites that were created in other software. Adobe Flash is the most common applications software used to create Flash files, but there are other software packages available.

Publishing a website on the Internet

When you create a website, you design and build all of the pages offline. You can view all of the pages in a web browser and see what they will look like and how all of the hyperlinks work just as if it was online. When you are happy that the website is finished, you need to upload the website files to an online server – this is often called posting a website.

The first step before posting a web page is to make sure you have some web space! You might get some free web space from your Internet service provider, or your school might provide some.

To publish a website online, you post the web pages that you have created to your web space along with any images used on the pages.

HTML

Most web-design software will code the website in HTML (hypertext mark-up language). You can design a website without ever seeing the HTML code behind it. For example, in Dreamweaver you can choose between **Design view** and **Code view**. Design view gives a view similar to how the final page looks in a web browser. This is known as **WYSIWYG**, which stands for 'what you see is what you get'. Some lines of the HTML from a web page are shown on the next page:

Did you know ??????

To view a website that is created in Flash, or that contains a Flash file, you need to have downloaded Flash player. This is a free piece of software (often referred to as a 'plug-in') and most websites that use Flash will also contain a link to download the Flash player.

Key terms

Flash: applications software used to add animation and interactivity to web pages.

Hotspots: areas of a page that change when the mouse hovers over or clicks on them. A hotspot can be invisible, for example an area of an image that does not immediately look as if it is clickable.

WYSIWYG: an acronym for 'what you see is what you get'. It is a term used to describe software that allows the user to view something very similar to the end result while the document is being edited.

Boost your grade!

Flash

Take a look at this website that was created entirely in Flash: **www.richardchasemore.com**. Now take a look at **www.nasa. gov/audience/forkids/kidsclub/ flash/index.html**. This website was created using HTML, but there are many Flash files within it. Notice how **hotspots** on the page change when you roll the mouse over them. There are also many animated effects on the page, and links to games that have been created using Flash.

```
<tr>
    <td height="220"> </td>
    <td valign="top"><!-- InstanceBeginEditable
name="MainEditRegion" -->
    <p class="style7 style16">&gt;Home</p>
    <p class="style7">Welcome to the <strong>Thai Cookery
School</strong>.</p>
    <p class="style7">We teach a variety of cookery courses
from complete beginners to seasoned chefs. All ages and abilities
welcome!</p>
    <p class="style7">Take a look at our courses to see upcoming
course details and dates.</p>
    <!-- InstanceEndEditable --></td>
    <td> </td>
</tr>
```

Web developers will often develop the website in a WYSIWYG editor (for example Design view in Dreamweaver), then switch to Code view to modify it. There are many reasons why you would want to edit the HTML directly. Here are some examples:

- to delete any unnecessary code that the WYSIWYG editor has added. This reduces the file size.
- to add HTML code, for example code that makes it easier for search engines to track your website, or free code that you have downloaded to insert a website counter.

Thai Cookery School

Home Courses Contact Photos Links

Welcome to the **Thai Cookery School**.

We teach a variety of cookery courses from complete beginners to seasoned chefs. All ages and abilities welcome!

Take a look at our courses to see upcoming course details and dates.

Thai Cookery School, The Old Mill, Tuddenham, IP7 3YY

 The web page created from the HTML text shown above left

Summary questions ✓

Thai Cookery School has a simple website shown in Screenshot **G**.

1 Which page is shown?

2 The website uses a template. Which parts of the page do you think are part of the template (and therefore are the same on every page of the website)?

3 How many pages in total do you think the website has? List the page names.

4 How many different text style types are used on the Home page (including those in the template)?

5 What is a website counter and where would you choose to put this on the page?

6 Suggest three ways you could use Flash to create an attention-grabbing effect.

7 Describe two steps you would take to post the website on the Internet.

3.6   Software for audio, DVD and video players

Windows Media Player and RealPlayer are examples of applications software that plays music and video, but there are many others. All of these have features such as:

- play, pause, forward and rewind
- volume adjustment and mute.

Play lists

Most applications software that plays music will let you create a **play list**. A play list is a selection of songs chosen by you from a library of music that the software will play in the order you specify. You can create a play list then burn that play list to a CD, save the play list for later or just use it to select which songs the computer will play next.

Music downloads

A music download is any piece of music that you have transferred from an online website to a local computer. There are many music download sites such as Apple iTunes, Amazon MP3 and eMusic where you pay to download a single track or album instead of buying a music CD.

H   Microsoft Media Player

Some download websites allow users to illegally download copyrighted music without permission. Preventing illegal downloads is something that record companies are working to try to stop!

Streaming

Music and video files tend to be quite large, so they can take a long time to download. **Streaming** allows a song or film that you are downloading to start playing before it has fully downloaded. The idea is that by the time you have watched or listened to the first few seconds of the downloaded file, a bit more will have been downloaded that you can then view or listen to. Websites such as YouTube use streaming. You may have experienced a video file stopping momentarily. This is because you are watching the film faster than it can be downloaded, so it needs a few seconds to catch up.

> ### Key terms
>
> **Play list**: a list of songs selected from a library.
>
> **Streaming**: multimedia content is played back to the end user whilst it is still being downloaded.

Summary questions

Mark each of these statements as true or false:

1. Streaming allows you to start listening to a music download before it has finished downloading.

2. Streaming is only suitable for small files.

3. A slow Internet connection when streaming will cause a film to pause often.

One of the features of applications software is the ability to transfer data from one application to another. Text can be transferred from a website to a presentation and to a DTP or word-processing file. Photos, graphics and even video can be transferred between different types of application software.

Files created using applications software are of a specific file type. For example, a word-processing document may have the file extension .doc, whilst a spreadsheet will have a file extension .xls. If you try to use word-processing software to open a spreadsheet file with the .xls extension, you will get an error! See Chapter 1, page 11 for more information on file extensions.

However, it is possible to transfer files between certain applications using the **import** and **export** features.

Here are some examples of which files types can be transferred:

- Word-processing documents with the extension .doc can be saved as .html files, and can then be edited in website design software.
- Images created using Photoshop that have the extension .psp can be exported as .jpg files. They can then be inserted into many other applications such as word-processing, presentation or desktop publishing software.
- Spreadsheet files can be exported as .csv files (comma separated values), which can be opened by a variety of different applications software including word-processing software.

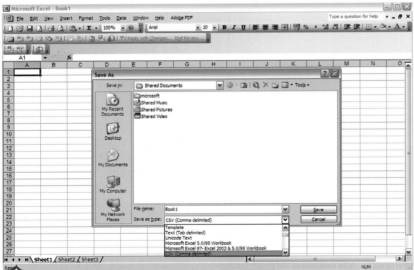

1 *Spreadsheet files can be saved as .csv files*

Key terms

Import: transfer a file that was created in one applications software package into the applications software that is currently open.

Export: preparing a file that is currently open so that it can be opened in different applications software.

AQA Examiner's tip

Data files in common text or graphic formats (for example .txt, .doc, .jpg, .csv) can be transferred between applications. They can be transferred by drag and drop or using an insert feature from a menu.

Summary questions

Mark each of these statements as true or false:

1. Files created using one type of applications software can be exported as different file types for use in different applications software.

2. Sound files cannot be opened using a word-processing package, even using export and import features.

3. If you want to change the file extension of a file, you can just rename it instead of using the import and export feature.

3.8 Designing documents using accepted layout

Before you begin creating a new document, you should consider if there is an accepted layout that you should use. These accepted layouts are to help other people read and understand your documents easily.

You should also consider if what you are creating is fit for the purpose and relevant to your audience. There would be no point in writing a presentation to wish someone well if they were ill. However, you might design a 'get well soon' card using graphics software.

Depending on which type of document you are creating – whether it is a letter, poster, presentation, etc. – there are some general rules about the format of the document. You need to be aware of these:

- **Printed letters**: usually contain the address of the recipient and the sender, the date and an appropriate sign-off. Each of these is found in a specific place on the page. It is rare to find an official letter that does not follow the traditional format.

- **Posters and flyers**: keep to one clear message using a simple, short title. Do not get carried away with many different colours, fonts and effects, as it will become cluttered and difficult to read.

- **Web page**: each web page should be clearly labelled so that a user knows at a glance which page they are currently on. It should also contain a navigation bar, which should be in the same location on each page.

- **Presentations:** do not fill each page with too much text. Stick to a small number of bullet points. Use images and multimedia content to add interest but without making the presentation too cluttered to understand.

In this chapter you will have learnt:

✔ the generic features found in most applications software

✔ the features common to word processors and desktop publishers

✔ when to choose a word processor and when to choose a desktop publisher for a given task

✔ the features found in presentation software

✔ which features to use to make a presentation interactive and multimedia

✔ which features are found in graphics production and image manipulation software, and how they are used to create and edit images

✔ the main features of web-design software such as hyperlinks, publishing online and including Flash animation

✔ the features of audio, DVD and video software

✔ that data can be transferred between applications

✔ that there are accepted layouts for many types of document.

AQA *Examiner's tip*

Many documents have an accepted layout (for example a business letter). Applications software (such as a word processor) usually provide templates for a variety of documents.

Summary questions ✔

Below is a list of guidelines for designing various types of documents. Match each rule to one of the document types listed above:

1 Use one simple title or headline, and do not try to include too much information.

2 Use short bullet points that are large and easy to read.

3 Display the page name clearly.

4 Use only one font, and keep to a traditional layout.

AQA Examination-style questions 🔑

1　Choose your answers from the **list given below**.

- A　Alteration of margins and spacing
- B　Complex searches on two or more criteria
- C　Number scales on axis to be edited
- D　Formatting of cells
- E　Construction of bar-charts and pie-charts from tables of data
- F　Sections of a picture to be copied, reflected and scaled
- G　Tables to be linked together
- H　Use of brushes
- I　Use of tabulation
- J　Validation of data

(a)　Which two of the above are important features that any word-processing package should allow? *(2 marks)*

(b)　Which two of the above are important features that a charts package should allow? *(2 marks)*

(c)　Which two of the above are important features that a graphics package should allow? *(2 marks)*

(d)　Give two of the above which are important features that any spreadsheet package should allow. *(2 marks)*

AQA, June 2007

2　Some types of applications software are **more suitable** than others for carrying out a given task.

- A　Database
- B　Desktop publishing
- C　Graphics
- D　Web design
- E　Word processing

Match the **best** type of applications software, A, B, C, D or E to carry out the tasks below.

(a)　Typing in, formatting and checking the text for a new novel

(b)　Designing the cover for a music CD

(c)　Storing and processing the details of members of a gym

(d)　Creating a printed school magazine that includes images of the various school activities over the year. *(4 marks)*

3　Below is a list of various types of applications software.

- A　Database
- B　Desktop publishing
- C　Drawing
- D　Mail-merging
- E　Modelling
- F　Spreadsheet
- G　Web design
- H　Word processing

Which **one** would be the **most suitable** to use for each of the following tasks?

(a)　Rotation of shapes

(b)　Typing in text for a novel

(c)　Using frames to position text and graphics on a page

(d)　Replication of cells

(e)　Carrying out a complex search on two or more criteria

(f)　A simple flight simulation. *(6 marks)*

AQA, June 2008

4　A graphic artist specialises in producing the artwork for comics and graphics novels. He uses a PC and a graphics package to produce his images. Which **two** of the following are important features that you would expect to find in a graphics package?

- A　Calculating the cost of each page of artwork
- B　Importing images
- C　Mail-merging letters
- D　Extensive search facilities
- E　Freehand drawing

(2 marks)

AQA, June 2007

5   Phantastic Phones sell mobile phones and accessories. The manager has produced the following leaflet using word-processing software. The leaflet will be given out to people shopping in the High Street.

> **Phantastic Phones Special Offers**
>
> To celebrate the end of our first year in business, we are offering these special deals.
>
> 1 Buy any new phone in May and get 25% off the marked price.
> 2 Take out a new monthly contract with us and get the first three months free.
>
> To reserve your phone or to get more details, phone Steve on 057 117 11700.

(a) Which of the following features of a word-processing package could be used to improve the **layout** of the leaflet?

A   Line spacing   B   Search facility   C   Mail-merging

D   Centre   E   Hyperlink   *(2 marks)*

(b) Give **two** additional features of a word-processing package that could be used to improve the **presentation** of the leaflet.   *(2 marks)*

(c) Give **one** feature of the software that could be used to check the accuracy of the text used in the leaflet.   *(1 mark)*

(d) The manager wants to use the word-processing package to rearrange the leaflet so that the second special deal comes before the first. Using the list given below, write down the steps needed to do this.

A   Paste   B   Cut

C   Highlight the second special deal   D   Position the cursor just above the
                                                  first special deal   *(2 marks)*

AQA, June 2006

6   **(a)** Why does web design software include 'publishing' features?   *(2 marks)*

(b) Give three other **specialist** features of web design software that could be used to build a website.   *(3 marks)*

7   A teacher is creating a presentation about climate change for use in a school assembly. She intends to use clip art in the presentation.

(a) Which one of the following **best** describes clip art?

A   A set of free software   B   Part of a computerised picture

C   A ready-made piece of computerised graphic art

D   A graphics tool from a graphic software gallery   *(1 mark)*

(b) The ability to use clip art and digital images is one feature of presentation software that can improve the appearance of a presentation. Give **three** other features of presentation software that could be used to improve the appearance of the school assembly presentation. *(3 marks)*

(c) What are the advantages of producing a report about climate change using presentation software compared with using DTP (desktop publishing)?   *(3 marks)*

8   **(a)** Which one of the following **best** describes media streaming?

A   Storing digital video and sound locally

B   The transmission of a set of digital figures

C   The transmission and viewing of digital video without first storing it

D   The transmission and local storage of digital sound   *(1 mark)*

(b) Describe two advantages of media streaming.   *(2 marks)*

(c) Describe a disadvantage of media streaming.   *(1 mark)*

4 Applications software 2

4.1 Spreadsheets and modelling software

Spreadsheets and **databases** are types of applications software used to store, manipulate and output information and data.

Almost every company in the world uses spreadsheets to make income and expense projections and to analyse company performance. A spreadsheet enables numbers to be processed and to be shown graphically if needed, making it easy for people to make decisions based on the information shown.

Databases are used to store data and to make that data easily accessible to users. The largest database in the world contains over 250 TB of data, and any one piece of data can be retrieved instantly.

Information and data

There is an important distinction between **information** and **data**. Data is raw figures or words with no context, for example: 2, Mid, V10, 5.2, 8, 560, 202, 165,000.

Data can be turned into information by giving it meaning. The Lamborghini Gallardo statistics in Table **A** are information. The same is true in a database or spreadsheet – without correct labelling the numbers and text stored within it would be meaningless!

Features of a spreadsheet

Data formats

A spreadsheet is typically used to store numerical data and to perform various calculations on that data. Spreadsheets deal with a large variety of **data types** and **number formats**. Look at Screenshot **C** which is an entry form for a football tournament. Various data types have been used.

There are more options that you can choose for number formats, such as number of decimal places, currency from many different countries, and fractions.

As with other applications software that you have used, such as word-processing software, you can use various formatting features to make the spreadsheet more presentable and easier to read, for example:

- font size and style
- text alignment
- merging cells
- cell shading and borders
- including gridlines
- column and row width.

A *Lamborghini Gallardo statistics*

Seats:	2
Engine position:	Mid
Engine type:	V10
Engine size:	5.2
0–100 mph:	8 seconds
Power:	560 bhp
Top speed:	202 mph
Retail price:	£165,000

B *Lamborghini Gallardo*

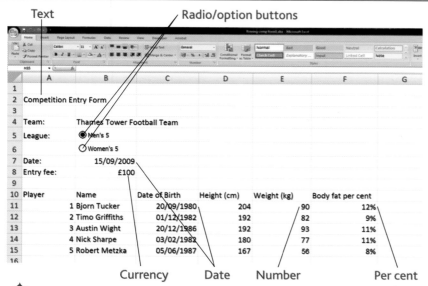

Text   Radio/option buttons

Currency   Date   Number   Per cent

 Entry form for football tournament showing data types and number formats

Key terms

Information: data with meaning.

Data: raw figures or words with no context or meaning.

Data types: descriptions of the types of data being stored in a cell, for example text, numbers or dates.

Number formats: descriptions of how the data in a cell is displayed, for example number of decimal places.

Functions: mathematical operations performed on the value in a cell, for example SUM and AVERAGE.

Cell references

Every cell in the spreadsheet has a unique address, known as a cell reference. A cell reference consists of a letter which specifies which column the cell is in, followed by a number which represents the row it is in. For example, in Screenshot **C**, the team name appears in cell B4.

You can also refer to a range of cells, for example D11:D15 means all of the cells from D11 to D15 inclusive, nine cells in total. This is particularly useful with **functions** such as SUM and AVERAGE which you will use later.

Boost your grade!

Referencing from different files

It is possible to reference a cell from a worksheet in a different file. You do this using the following format – listing first the file name, then the sheet number, and finally the cell column and row:

'[Football.xls]Sheet1'!E26

This is the complete cell reference for cell E26, which is on Sheet1 in the file Football.xls.

■ Formulae and functions

Spreadsheets are mainly used to enter numbers and then perform calculations on them. Look at the spreadsheet in Screenshot **D** (overleaf) on the next page. It was created to calculate how much profit was made from a charity cream tea stall at the school fête.

Every number highlighted in Screenshot **D** has been automatically calculated by the spreadsheet. One of the advantages of using formulae in this way is that if you change one small thing such as the quantity of tea sold, all of the other cells are automatically updated to reflect this change.

Activity 4.1

Formatting a spreadsheet

Create the spreadsheet shown in Screenshot **C**. Make sure each cell has the correct data type.

Use the features listed at the bottom of page 56 to make the entry form more presentable. Save the spreadsheet to use later.

Did you know ??????

Radio buttons (also called option buttons) are used where only one option in a list can be selected. If you want people to be able to select more than one item in a list, you should use check boxes.

Remember

Cell references always contain a letter followed by a number, for example A5 – never the other way around! If you write 6B when you mean B6 this will be marked as wrong in an examination.

Activity 4.2

Using formulae

1 Create the cream tea spreadsheet in Screenshot **D** using a spreadsheet package. Enter all of the numbers except the ones highlighted.

2 Now, enter a formula in D6 that multiplies the quantity of tea sold by the unit cost of tea (B6 × C6). If you are not sure how to enter a multiplication formula, look it up in the Help feature.

3 Copy and paste the formula in D6 to cells D7 and D8. Double check that the formulae have been transferred correctly.

The SUM function

When you have a long list of numbers to add together it is much better to use the **SUM** function than simple addition.

In the example given in Screenshot **D**, you need to add together the cost of all the ingredients in cells D12 to D18. Instead of writing =D12+D13+D14+D15+D16+D17+D18, you can use the SUM function and just write =SUM(D12:D18). This is much quicker and more efficient.

MIN, MAX and AVERAGE

Three other useful functions are **MIN**, **MAX** and **AVERAGE**. They are used to find the minimum value, maximum value and average of a list of numbers. You will use these functions to find the minimum weight, maximum weight and average weight of all the football players in the example given in Screenshot **C**.

The MIN function has the following format:

MIN (FirstValue:LastValue)

where FirstValue is the first cell reference in the list and LastValue is the last cell reference. MAX and AVERAGE functions follow the same format.

Activity 4.4

The MIN, MAX and AVERAGE functions

Using the football spreadsheet that you produced for Activity 4.1, add the following somewhere underneath the table:

- Minimum weight
- Maximum weight
- Average weight.

Enter the following as the formula for minimum weight: =MIN(E11:E15).

Now enter formulae for maximum weight and average weight.

	Player	Name	Date of Birth	Height (cm)	Weight (kg)	Body fat per cent
10						
11		1 Bjorn Tucker	20/09/1980	204	90	12%
12		2 Timo Griffiths	01/12/1982	192	82	9%
13		3 Austin Wight	20/12/1986	192	93	11%
14		4 Nick Sharpe	03/02/1982	180	77	11%
15		5 Robert Metzka	05/06/1987	167	56	8%
16						
17				Minimum weight:	56	
18				Maximum weight:	93	
19				Average weight:	80	

E *MIN, MAX and AVERAGE weights of the players*

	A	B	C	D
1				
2	**Cream Tea Stall**			
3				
4	**Sales:**			
5		Quantity sold	Cost	Total
6	Tea	37	£ 0.50	£ 18.50
7	Coffee	17	£ 0.75	£ 12.75
8	Cream scone	43	£ 2.70	£ 116.10
9			Total Sales	£ 147.35
10				
11	**Cost of Sales:**			
12	Tea		£	2.00
13	Coffee		£	3.00
14	Milk		£	5.00
15	Sugar		£	2.50
16	Scones		£	15.00
17	Jam		£	10.00
18	Cream		£	10.00
19			Total cost of sales:	£ 47.50
20				
21	**Profit:**			£ 99.85

 Profit from cream tea sales

Activity 4.3

The SUM function

Using the spreadsheet you produced for Activity 4.2, write a SUM function in cell D19 that adds together cells D12 to D18. Write another SUM function in cell D9 that adds together cells D6 to D8.

Enter a formula for Profit that is 'Total Sales – Total cost of sales'.

Other useful functions

There are many functions available in spreadsheet software. Table **F** shows a handful of other functions that you should be familiar with.

F *Useful functions*

Function name	Description	Example
ROUND	Rounds a number to a specified number of digits	=ROUND(D1,2) Rounds the number in cell D1 to 2 digits.
ROUND UP	Rounds a number UP	=ROUNDUP(D1,2) Rounds up the number in cell D1 to 2 digits.
RANK	Tells you the position of one number within a sequence of numbers	=RANK(D4,D4:D9) Tells you where the number in cell D4 ranks in the range of numbers in cells D4 to D9
COUNT	Counts the number of cells that contain numbers	=COUNT(D1:D10) Tells you how many of the cells in the range D1 to D10 contain numbers
LOOKUP	Looks up a number in an array (a type of table)	=LOOKUP("apple",A2:A6,B2:B6) Looks for the word 'apple' in column A cells 2 to 6 of the table, and shows the corresponding value in column B.

Boost your grade!

Relative and absolute cell references

Take a look at this example.

Liam lives at number 15 Graveney Road. Alex lives at number 16 Graveney Road. The two houses are opposite each other.

If you asked Alex where he lives, he could give either an absolute reference or a relative reference:

- an absolute reference would be: number 16 Graveney Road
- a relative reference would be: opposite to Liam.

In a spreadsheet, a **relative cell reference** means that, for example, cell D2 is three columns to the right and one row down. In Screenshot **E**, if the formula in D11 refers to the height of the first player, when this formula is copied down column D the cell reference needs to change to the next player. However, the cell reference for the average weight must not change!

If you do not want a cell reference to be changed, you need to use an **absolute cell reference**. You write an absolute cell reference using the $ character. If you want to refer to the average weight (in cell E19, Screenshot **E**) as an absolute reference you would write E19.

Look at the difference between a relative and absolute cell reference in a formula:

Relative reference: =IF(E11<E19, "UNDER", "OVER").

Absolute reference: =IF(E11<E19, "UNDER", "OVER").

Boost your grade!

The IF function

The **IF** function is used if you want the value in a cell to depend on the answer to a question. The IF statement needs to say: 'If weight is less than average, write UNDER, otherwise write OVER'. The function will look like this: IF(players weight<average weight, "UNDER", "OVER"). Translated into cell references this looks like: =IF(E11<E19, "UNDER", "OVER").

Key terms

IF: an IF statement asks a question, then returns one value if the answer is yes, and another if the answer is no.

Relative cell reference: where the program does not actually store the address of the cell. Instead it stores the position of the cell relative to the cell containing the formula.

Absolute cell reference: the actual location of the cell is stored, and is unaffected by the location of the cell containing the formula.

AQA Examiner's tip

Cells may contain different types of data (numbers, currency, text) or they may contain formulae (for example B3/C5) and functions (for example SUM(D2:D9)). Cells can also be formatted to have different styles (for example bold) and sizes (for example 16 point).

Sorting

A useful feature of a spreadsheet is the ability to immediately sort a table of data into a specific order.

The football spreadsheet is currently in order of player number. The sort feature would be used if you wanted to re-order the table. It is possible to sort on both text and numbers, so you could:

- sort the table alphabetically by player first name (if you wanted to sort by surname you would need to write the surname in a separate column)
- sort the table in order of height, with the tallest first.

Graphs and charts

There is a large variety of graphs and charts that you can create using spreadsheets. Based on the football spreadsheet in Screenshot **C** and the cream tea spreadsheet in Screenshot **D** you could create:

- a pie chart of all the ingredient costs
- a scattergram of the heights and weights of all the players
- a bar chart of the sales of tea, coffee and scones.

Chart titles, labels and keys

It is important to make sure that all charts and graphs are properly labelled. Depending on what sort of graph or chart you have created, it will need:

- a chart title
- a key (sometimes called a legend) that explains what the colours or symbols on the chart represent
- axis titles
- appropriate axis scales.

Modelling

Spreadsheets can be used to model situations, allowing you to change various values and see what the effect is.

Use the cream tea spreadsheet in Screenshot **D** as an example. Imagine you are in a meeting discussing a future cream tea event at a school open day. Following the success of the first event, everyone is confident that profits could be improved for the next event. The main issues that arise are:

- How much would you have to charge per scone to generate a profit of £100?
- To make it easier to handle the money on the day, the organisers would like to change the price of tea, coffee and scones to £1 each. Assuming the number sold remains the same, what is the effect on the profit?
- What is the effect on profit if the price of coffee is reduced to 50p, and 25 cups of coffee are sold?

Each of these scenarios can be easily answered using the cream tea spreadsheet that you have already created.

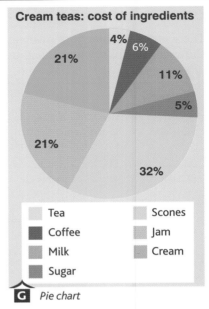

Cream teas: cost of ingredients

Tea	Scones
Coffee	Jam
Milk	Cream
Sugar	

G Pie chart

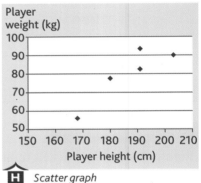

Player weight (kg)

Player height (cm)

H Scatter graph

To find the answer to the first example, you would try entering different values in the cream scone cost cell (**C8**). What scone cost gives a profit closest to £100? You are not expected to get the correct cost straight away – the idea is to use trial and improvement. If the profit is less than £100 you will need to increase the cost, and if it is over £100 you will need to reduce it.

Summary questions

1 Which of the following statements is true?

a Data + information = context

b Data + meaning = information

2 Sarah has created the following spreadsheet to estimate her monthly phone bill.

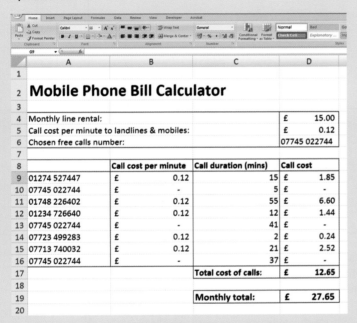

Which data formats are used in the following cells?

a A2

b D4

c A9.

3 Which of the following formulae would you use in cell D17?

a =D9+D10+D11+D12+D13+D14+D15+D16

b =SUM(D9+D16)

c =SUM(D9:D16).

4 The formula used in cell D9 is =B9*C9.

a Are the cell references in this formula relative or absolute?

b If the formula in cell D9 is copied and pasted into cell D10, what would it be?

c Write a formula, using the MAX function, that displays the longest call duration.

Boost your grade!

'What if'

Remember that there are three steps in the modelling process or 'what if' questions:

- reduce/increase a variable
- check result
- continue until the result is correct.

AQA Examiner's tip

In modelling, if you use the word 'change' you will not be awarded any marks. You need to be more specific with the language you use, for example 'increase' or 'reduce'.

Activity 4.6

Use a spreadsheet to model different scenarios

Using the cream tea spreadsheet from Activity 4.2, enter different values to reflect each of the three scenarios that are being discussed in the meeting. Model the best answer to each scenario. Write a brief sentence in response to each of the bullet points listed, stating what you would say in the meeting following your analysis.

AQA Examiner's tip

If you are asked to explain the difference between information and data in the exam, you will probably find it easiest to give some examples. The same is true for many of the features of spreadsheets and databases. If something is best explained with an example then use one!

4.2　Databases

A database is used for storing data in a highly efficient and organised way so that it can be easily and quickly retrieved. The simplest definition of a database is a structured collection of records. A small paper address book organised alphabetically is an example of a simple database. A stock system for a supermarket or an online encyclopaedia such as Wikipedia are examples at the larger end of the scale. The data for all of these examples is organised in such a way that it can be easily retrieved in a useful form.

Did you know ? ? ? ? ? ?

Imagine searching for a name in a phone book with a billion pages – that is what a database called ChoicePoint does. It can almost instantly return the details requested from a database that would reach to the moon and back if it was printed!

■ Types of data 🄺

As with spreadsheets, databases deal with a variety of different types of data.

Table **I** is a simple database used by the organiser of a rowing race to store data about all of the competitors.

I　A table of data for rowing races

BoatID	BoatName	Race	CoachName	RaceTime	FinishPosition	EntryFee	Paid?
29471	Titania	M	James Kapp			£250	Y
39975	Loyola	F	Emma Gilbertson			£200	Y
91320	Goldie	M	Roger Newcombe			£250	N

The race day has not yet taken place so there are no race times or finish positions. There will be two races, one for men and one for women. The Race column in the database specifies which race the boat is entered in.

J　Data types

Data type	Description
AutoNumber	Numbers that are automatically generated for each record. AutoNumber is normally used for key fields to make sure each one is different
Number	Numeric values. These can be integers or decimals
Alphanumeric/Text	Short values containing numbers and letters
Currency	Monetary values
Date/Time	Dates and times
Object/Image (sometimes called Attachment)	Files such as digital photos
Logical/Boolean	Yes/No values
Limited choice	Where values are limited to those in a drop-down list
Memo	Text and numbers. It is possible to store a large number of characters, for example you can use this for a 'Notes' or 'Description' field.

Activity 4.7

Choosing appropriate data types

The column headings in Table **I** represent the field names in the database. For each of the field names, choose an appropriate data type from Table **J**.

Data structures k!

A simple database is basically a table of data like that in Table **I**. A database that consists of just one table is called a **flat file database**. In a database, it is not correct to refer to columns and rows. Instead, the terms **fields** and **records** are used.

Each column heading represents a field in the database. There are eight fields in the rowing race database. Each row is a record in the database; there is one record per boat, and Table **I** has three records.

Problems with flat file databases

The main problem with flat file databases is the duplication of information. This duplication is known as **data redundancy**. Entering duplicates of the same data is time consuming and a waste of file space. It can also lead to a greater possibility of errors in the database. If the race organiser wanted to add the details of each member of the crew to the database in Table **I**, the flat file database would look like Table **K**.

> **Key terms**
>
> **Flat file database**: a database with just one table of data.
>
> **Fields**: column headings in database tables. Fields are part of a record.
>
> **Records**: these are also rows in a database table, and they hold all of the information about one subject.
>
> **Data redundancy**: when the same data is stored more than once in a table. This is sometimes called data duplication.

K   *Table of data for rowing race including crew details*

BoatID	BoatName	Race	CoachName	RaceTime	FinishPosition	EntryFee	Paid?	RowerName	DateOfBirth
29471	Titania	M	James Kapp			£250	Y	Cameron Davies	4/8/79
29471	Titania	M	James Kapp			£250	Y	Vikram Seth	25/1/69
29471	Titania	M	James Kapp			£250	Y	Andrew Gates	16/9/90
29471	Titania	M	James Kapp			£250	Y	Mike Ross	21/10/91
39975	Loyola	F	Emma Gilbertson			£200	Y	Alex Lamb	4/8/79
39975	Loyola	F	Emma Gilbertson			£200	Y	Claire Fernandis	9/5/81
39975	Loyola	F	Emma Gilbertson			£200	Y	Steph McFarlane	1/11/88
39975	Loyola	F	Emma Gilbertson			£200	Y	Katie Robinson	25/1/69
91320	Goldie	M	Roger Newcombe			£250	N	Robert Metzka	16/9/90
91320	Goldie	M	Roger Newcombe			£250	N	Bjorn Tucker	21/10/91
91320	Goldie	M	Roger Newcombe			£250	N	Craig Harley	1/11/88
91320	Goldie	M	Roger Newcombe			£250	N	Austin Wright	9/5/81

Notice that the boat details such as **BoatID**, **BoatName**, and **CoachName** have to be typed in for every boat member. When the race organiser enters the race times and positions, they will have to enter them four times, once for each rower! This information should only need to be entered once.

> AQA **Examiner's tip**
>
> Removing redundant data (duplicated data) makes data entry faster and more accurate and reduces storage space.

Relational databases

To overcome the problems of data redundancy that you get with flat file databases, you can use more than one table. There will be one table for the boat information and another for rowers. Both tables will be linked.

A database that contains linked tables is called a **relational database**.
The two tables will look like this.

Boat table:

Field name	Data type
BoatID	AutoNumber
BoatName	Text
Race	Text
CoachName	Text
RaceTime	Time
FinishPosition	Number
EntryFee	Currency
Paid?	Y/N

Rower table:

Field name	Data type
RowerID	AutoNumber
BoatID	Number
RowerName	Text
DateOfBirth	Date
Photo	attachment

The race organiser could also add a Photo field with the data type 'attachment' if he needed photo ID for all the entrants.

 L *Example of a relational database*

The tables will be linked using the **BoatID** field.

Key fields

All tables in a database should have a **key field** (also known as a primary key). The key field must be unique. For example, it would be a bad idea to make **BoatName** a key field in Diagram **L** because there is a chance that two boats will have the same name. For this reason an additional field called **BoatID** is used. The same is true for the Rower table in Diagram **L**.

Forms

You can enter boat and crew details directly into the tables, but it is much more convenient to use database input forms. The Boat form (Screenshot **M**) contains all of the fields from the Boat table (Table **L**) in the same order as they appear in the Boat table.

Advantages of using a form

A form is used to simplify data entry. Forms make it easier to enter data:

- They allow you to enter data into more than one table using a single form. In the example of the rowing race, it would be possible to create a form that allowed you to enter data into the Boat table and the Rower table at the same time.

- Forms give you many layout options, and look much more user friendly than tables.

- You can add extra text to a form to make it more user friendly.

M A database form

Boat Form	
BoatID	1
BoatName	Titania
Race:	M
CoachName	James Kapp
RaceTime	
FinishPosition	
EntryFee	£250.00
Paid?	☑

Record: 1 of 3   No Filter   Search

Sorting and filters

You can sort the data in tables **and** reports using a method that is similar to the way you sort tables in a spreadsheet. You can sort in ascending or descending order, and you can also sort using more than one field.

Examples of sorts you could do are:

- Sort the Boat table (Diagram **L**) in order of race time. You would use an ascending sort on the RaceTime field to do this.

- Separate the results of the men's and women's race. You could sort first by race type (M or F), and then by race time. To do this you would use an ascending or descending sort on the Race field, and then an ascending sort on the RaceTime field.

Filtering allows you to select information on one particular type of data. If you want to enter the race positions in the men's race you would filter using the Race type field and select M. This would show only the boats in the men's race, allowing for easy entry of positions.

Searching a database

One of the most powerful features of a database is the ability to search and find specific information.

You can set search criteria, then the database very quickly searches through all of the records in the database (which might be millions) and returns only the results you are looking for.

Setting search criteria

To tell the database which records you are looking for, you need to set search criteria. Examples of searches you might want to do on the Race database are:

- find all rowing teams who have not paid their race entry fee
- find all boats who completed the race in less than four minutes
- find all rowers who are younger than 16 years old
- find all boats who are not coached by James Kapp.

To do those searches, you need to design a database query and enter the search criteria using the symbols shown in Table **N**.

N Search criteria

Search criteria		Table and field that the database criteria applies to	Example
=	equals	Paid? field in the Boat table (Diagram **L**)	Paid? = "N"
<	less than	RaceTime field in the Boat table	RaceTime < 4:00
>	more than	DateOfBirth field in the Rower table (Diagram **L**)	DateOfBirth > 9/1/1993 (this will depend on the current date)
<>	not equal	Coach field in the Boat table	Coach <> "James Kapp"

Reports

One of the most useful features of a database is the ability to run reports on the data. Reports can be based on one table in the database, or they can contain data from multiple tables.

When you create a report, you can select which fields to show and also what order and layout to present the results in. Reports can also be linked to searches, filters and sorts. If you have designed a search or sort you can then use a report to present the data so that it is easy to understand.

Examples of reports that the race organiser can run using the information in the database are:

- a list of boats in time order
- a contact sheet listing all of the coaches, the boat they represent and their contact numbers
- a report of every boat that has not yet paid their entry fee, and how much the entry fee is for that boat.

Boost your grade!

Advanced search criteria

It is possible to set more complicated criteria, where the database searches many fields in the database. These searches would require the database to search more than one field:

- Find all boats in the men's race with a race time of less than four minutes. This would involve both the Race field and the RaceTime field in the Boat table (Diagram **L**).
- Find all boats that EITHER completed the race in less than four minutes OR that had a finish position of less than five. This would involve both the RaceTime field and the FinishPosition fields from the Boat table (Diagram **L**).

Did you know ??????

You can use wildcards when entering search criteria. For example, if you searched for all rowers with a name equal to g*, the database search would return all rowers whose names started with g.

Activity 4.9

Reports

For each of the reports listed (left), state which fields you would use from each table in the database from Diagram **L** on page 64.

AQA Examiner's tip

Learn the following things about reports. When creating a report the user can:

- select the fields to display
- choose the order that the fields appear in
- add header/footer information for each page of the report.

MD Frames Limited

MD Frames is a small family-run framing company. Customers bring in prints, paintings or photos, and MD Frames make a custom frame to fit. Until recently they were using a paper order book, but they were finding this often caused problems:

- Some customers dropped off their prints for framing then did not collect them for months. MD Frames had no way of tracking these customers without manually going through the order book.

- Some customers brought in many prints, but each time they placed an order, the staff at MD Frames would have to write down their contact details on the order form again. This was time consuming and annoyed the customers!

The solution was to create a database that contained all of the customer information, codes for common frame types and a log of every order placed by each customer. Later MD Frames added fields for the order status, invoice amount and amount due. This is a good example of the use of ICT to solve a problem.

Boost your grade!

Archiving data

In a database such as the one that MD Frames uses, the data held in it is constantly increasing, so the database ends up holding a large amount of data that is no longer needed. The solution to this is to archive the data. It is possible in a database program to run a report that automatically archives off data that matches specific criteria (for example orders older than five years).

AQA **Examiner's tip**

Reports can also include merged data from several files/tables.

Mail merge

A mail merge allows the data stored in a database to be transferred to another type of application software such as a word processor or an e-mail. Common uses of a mail merge are:

- A mail merge that selects all customers who have placed an order in the last six months, alerting them to a special promotion. The name and contact information of the customers stored in the database would automatically be linked to the word-processed document. The word processor would then create letters to be sent to the customers, making the whole process automated.

- A mail merge that prints a specific customer's details on a customer loyalty card. The customer name (taken from the database) and the date the card was issued are printed on the membership card automatically.

- A mail merge that is used to send out payslips to all of the staff at the end of the month. The database contains the name and contact details of all the staff. The monthly wages and tax information is inserted and then all of the payslip letters are printed in one batch and sent out.

Activity 4.10

Mail merge

Think of three more applications of mail merge for the company MD Frames featured in the case study above.

Here you select which fields you want to appear in the mail merge. The fields from the contact list you selected will appear here, and you choose from these. The merge fields selected in this example are highlighted grey.

You can choose to type in all the contact details for the mail merge, use existing e-mail contacts you have stored, or an existing database of contacts/customers.

You can use a letter that is already written, or type a new one for the mail merge.

O *Mail merge in Microsoft Word*

Summary questions ✔

A school head of year creates a simple database that contains details of all pupils in the year. The details held about each pupil are: PupilName, ParentContact, Address, FormNumber. There are six Form groups in the year, and the FormNumber relates to which Form group a pupil is in.

1 The database consists of just one table called Pupil. What would the key field be in the Pupil table? Is there a suitable field mentioned above or would a new field need to be created?

2 What data type would you use for the key field and why?

3 The head of year now wants to add details of each form tutor and form room number. What potential problems could be caused if these details are added to the Pupil table?

4 What search criteria would you use to find all pupils who are either in Form 1 or Form 2?

In this chapter you will have learnt:

✔ the difference between data and information, and the relationship between the two

✔ which features and functions are found in spreadsheet software, and how these are used

✔ how a spreadsheet is used to model 'what if' scenarios

✔ how to design a database, and the problems caused by data redundancy

✔ how to search and filter information in a database

✔ how database reports can be used to summarise data in a database.

AQA Examination-style questions 🔲

1   **(a)**   Which type of applications software is often used for financial modelling?   *(1 mark)*

     (b)   Applications software can be used for modelling a variety of situations. Explain briefly what is meant by the term **modelling**.   *(2 marks)*

AQA, June 2007

2   Some students are planning a School Prom for Year 11. Their first attempt is shown below.

	A	B	C	D	E
1	Year 11 Prom Planner				
2					
3	29 June 2008				
4					
5	Number of students paying	150			
6					
7	**Expenditure**	**Cost of each**	**Number needed**	**Total Cost**	
8	Coach Hire	£75.00	4	£300.00	
9	Function rooms	£100.00	3	£300.00	
10	Decorations (per room)	£22.50	3	£67.50	
11	Three course meal	£14.00	150	£2,100.00	
12	Soft drinks	£3.50	150	£525.00	
13					
14					
15					
16					
17	**Total cost of the Prom**			£3,292.50	
18					
19	**Cost per student**			£21.95	

   (a)   What is the cell reference of the shaded cell?   *(1 mark)*

   (b)   Name **three** cell formats that have been used in this spreadsheet.   *(3 marks)*

   (c)   A spreadsheet can generate different types of graph. Give **one** suitable type of graph that could be used to display the various kinds of expenditure.   *(1 mark)*

   (d)   What formula has been used to calculate the cost per student in D19?   *(1 mark)*

   (e)   Many Year 11 students said that the maximum they would pay to go to the Prom would be £20. Explain how the software could be used for modelling situations, to try to keep the cost under £20.   *(2 marks)*

AQA, June 2008

3   A video shop stores information about its customers in a database table.
Part of the customer database table is given below.

ID Number	Surname	First name	House No.	Postcode	Date of Birth
0021	Jones	Jon	6	ZZ23 2KJ	20/11/80
0034	Smith	Anne	78	ZZ20 3GT	12/08/75
0156	Ali	Ahmed	17	ZZ16 1KN	06/02/82
0234	Collins	Sarah	2	ZZ23 4PH	31/01/70
0452	Chan	Michael	113	ZZ12 8PR	15/10/84

(a) How many records are shown in this database table?   *(1 mark)*

(b) Which is the key field in this database table?   *(1 mark)*

(c) Which **one** of the following is the best definition of a key field?
   A   A key field must be the first field in a customer database table
   B   A key field must be a combination of letters and numbers
   C   A key field must be unique in a database table   *(1 mark)*

(d) As well as the customer table, the video store uses two other linked tables. Name **one** other table it would be sensible for them to use.   *(1 mark)*

(e) Give **one** reason why the video store should link tables together.   *(1 mark)*

AQA, June 2007

4   CottagesRUS is a company that rents out holiday homes. They use a database to store information on their properties to rent. Part of the Database file is shown below.

Property ID	Type of Property	Property location	Max people	Heating	Weekly rent (min-max)	Pets allowed
C4UC01	C	Lancre	4	CH	£200 - £300	Y
C4UC02	C	Lancre	4	CF	£200 - £300	N
C4UH02	H	Hickley	12	CH	£300 - £500	N
C4UC04	C	Hickley	6	EF	£250 - £375	N
C4UB02	B	Lancre	6	CH	£275 - £375	N
C4UB03	B	Hickley	4	CH	£175 - £275	Y
C4UH03	H	Lancre	8	CH	£300 - £400	Y
C4UC06	C	Lancre	6	CF	£200 - £300	N
C4UC07	C	Lancre	2	CH	£150 - £225	N
C4UH05	H	Hickley	8	CH	£250 - £375	N
C4UB05	B	Hickley	4	CH	£175 - £250	Y
C4UC09	C	Lancre	2	CH	£150 - £225	Y

The following codes have been used for the **Type of Property** field.
C – Cottage
H – House
B – Bungalow

(a) Name **one** other field that has been coded.   *(1 mark)*

(b) How many records are shown in this database file?   *(1 mark)*

(c) Why is the Property ID field needed? *(1 mark)*

(d) Which one of the following is an important reason why CottagesRUS uses data validation to check the data as it is entered into the database?

    A   Make sure that it is correct

    B   Make sure that it is sensible

    C   Make sure that it is sorted into order   *(1 mark)*

(e) Which field would be the most suitable to validate using a range check?

    A   Property location

    B   Max people

    C   Heating   *(1 mark)*

(f) Give **two** advantages to CottagesRUS of using a database rather than a manual method for storing this information.   *(2 marks)*

(g) Write down the **Property ID(s)** found as a result of the following searches.

    A   Search 1: **Max people** equal to 12

    B   Search 2: **Property location** equal to Lancre AND **Pets allowed** equal to Y

    C   Search 3: **Heating** NOT equal to CH   *(3 marks)*

AQA, June 2008

5 Using the web

5.1 Web browsing and e-mail

Over the past few years there has been a huge change in the way people communicate online. Now most people not only have an e-mail account, they have profiles on social networking sites and their own personal blogs, and they may regularly use and contribute to Internet forums. This chapter looks at each of these online tools and how they are used by both individuals and companies.

■ Web browsers 🎮

A **web browser** (also called an Internet browser) is the software used to look at web pages. You will almost certainly have used one before. Two of the most common web browsers are Microsoft Internet Explorer and Mozilla Firefox. Web browsers have many useful features for navigating to web pages.

Objectives

Become familiar with e-mail, web-browser software, search engines and search terms.

Know what is meant by a social networking site, web log and a forum, and how individuals and organisations use them.

Understand what a podcast is, and know that different types of podcast are available.

Stop: Use the Stop button if you want the browser to stop loading a page, for example if it is taking a long time, or if you have accidentally clicked a link.

Refresh: Refresh reloads the current web page. This is useful for web pages that update regularly – for example an online e-mail inbox, or news feed.

Key terms

Web browser: also called an Internet browser. It is a software application used to view web pages.

Web address: Every web page has an address. It usually begins with 'www'. In a web browser, you type the web-page address that you want to view into the address bar and (provided you are online!) the web page is displayed.

Home page: A web browser allows you to set a Home page. This is the web page address that the browser will automatically navigate to each time you open it and each time you press the Home icon.

A The Nelson Thornes home page viewed in Microsoft Internet Explorer

Pop-ups

Pop-ups are additional browser windows that are opened by the web page that you are currently viewing. Sometimes these are desirable – for example, if you are browsing the web page of a theme park and you click to open another window that shows a map of the park. More annoyingly many websites open pop-up windows containing advertisements.

Most web browsers have an option that lets you block pop-ups, or asks your permission before opening a pop-up.

Favourites and bookmarks

To save you from typing in the web address of your favourite websites each time you want to open them, you can set up a list of favourites (also called bookmarks). There is no limit to the number of favourites you can specify, and you can also organise them into folders and subfolders just as you can when saving other types of file. To go to one of your favourite websites, you just select it from a menu in the browser.

■ Common types of website

Search engines

Examples of search engines are Google, Yahoo! Search, and Ask. Search engines work by searching through all of the pages on the Internet and making a central index of words and sentences on each web page. When you enter a word or sentence into a search engine, the search engine looks up the word or string of words in its central index and returns a list of all the websites that contain that word or sequence of words. Different search engines use different methods for indexing websites, so they will return different results for the same search terms.

Entering search criteria **k!**

When you enter a few words into a search engine, it returns the websites that contain those words most frequently.

It is also possible to enter multiple search criteria, and to specify in more detail the sort of results you are searching for. Look at the examples in Table **B**.

B *Examples of detailed search criteria*

Type of search criteria	Example search criteria	Finds pages containing
AND search – simply type in the search terms	hotel London	the words **hotel** AND **London**
NOT search – often involves putting a minus sign (–) before a search term	MP3 player – iPod	**MP3** players but NOT **iPods**
OR search – using the word **OR** between two search terms	Cornwall windsurfing OR wakeboarding	information on **Cornwall windsurfing** OR **Cornwall wakeboarding**
Exact phrase – putting search terms in quotes (" ")	"let me entertain you"	the exact phrase '**let me entertain you**'
Wildcard search – using an asterisk * before or after a search term.	Cook*	Words beginning with **Cook**, for example **cook, cooking, cooks, cookery, cooker**

Remember

Millions of keywords are stored in a search engine's central index. You need to think carefully about the words you use for your search. Imagine you want to make some bread. Try entering the word 'bread' into a search engine. There are millions of hits, including a 1970s rock band, an old TV programme and a credit card. Search for 'wholemeal bread recipe' and the number of results has reduced substantially.

AQA Examiner's tip

Learn the ways of setting search criteria:

- a simple search
- narrow two criteria using AND
- combine two criteria using OR
- remove some aspects of the criteria using NOT
- include a wildcard to find links which are like the one typed in.

Did you know ??????

Google does not actually use asterisks (or wildcards). If you search for 'cook', Google will automatically include related terms such as *cooks* and *cooking* in the search results.

Wiki

Wiki is the name given to sites that allow users to freely create and edit webpage content using a web browser. The most well-known example of a wiki site is Wikipedia, the online encyclopedia. Anyone can log on to Wikipedia and create a page on a new subject, or go to an existing page and add content and links, or edit content that is currently there. For more information about how people use wikis see Chapter 9, page 126.

Internet service providers

An **Internet service provider (ISP)** is a company that connects people to the Internet. ISPs usually charge a monthly fee in return for providing Internet access. This may be via a variety of connection types such as dial-up connection, cable, wireless or broadband.

Customers are normally required to sign up to the ISP for a minimum length of time (12 or 18 months is common).

Many ISPs provide other services in addition to providing Internet access, such as web mail and website hosting. You may also have seen companies offering a phone line and digital TV as part of the same package.

Web mail

The ISP may provide you with one or more free e-mail addresses and an online account. You can log into the online account and check your messages. The e-mail account will come with a certain amount of free storage, so you can store e-mails online up to that limit.

Hosting a website

Some ISPs provide free web space. This means that if you create your own website using website design software, you can upload it to your free web space and have a live website! The ISP will provide you with the details needed to upload or post your web pages.

E-mail 🎴

There are many different e-mail providers. Popular examples are Hotmail, Gmail and AOL. All e-mail providers have the same common features that allow you to write e-mails and send and receive them. They also allow you to send and receive attached files (attachments) and keep an address book containing all of your contacts.

Sending e-mail

To send an e-mail to someone you need to have an e-mail account and know the e-mail address of the person that you want to write to.

Look at Screenshot **C**, which shows an e-mail from Daniel (the organiser of a rock-climbing club) to members of the club. The main features of the e-mail have been explained.

Receiving e-mail

Screenshot **D** is what the e-mail looks like when it is received by a club member.

⚭ links

Go to **www.wikipedia.org**. Click on English and then on the left menu click About Wikipedia – here there is lots of information about how users create and edit content.

Key terms

Internet service provider (ISP): a company that provides people with access to the Internet, for example using dial-up, cable or a broadband connection.

Boost your grade!

POP and SMTP

You may have come across POP and SMTP when sending and receiving e-mails.

POP stands for 'Post Office Protocol' and is the language used to send e-mail from an online server to your computer.

SMTP stands for 'Simple Mail Transfer Protocol'. This is the language used to send mail from your computer to an online mail server.

For example, if you have an e-mail program on your computer such as Microsoft Outlook, it will probably use POP to collect mail from an online e-mail server and put it in your inbox, and use SMTP to transfer e-mails you write to the online server and onto the recipient.

From: Some e-mail editing software lets you send and receive e-mails from more than one e-mail account. In that case you need to specify which account you are sending the e-mail from by entering an e-mail address into the **From** field.

Cc: This stands for **carbon copy**. It is used to send a copy of an e-mail to someone who is not directly affected by the message, but who you want to be aware of it. In this example the school head of year has been sent a copy so that she is aware there is no practice.

Subject: You should always enter a subject line that makes it clear what the e-mail is about, and will make it easy for recipients to find the e-mail if they need to refer back to it.

To: You can enter one e-mail address or many e-mail addresses to send your message to. List all of the addresses in the **To** field. You need to separate the e-mail addresses using either a comma or a semi-colon depending on which e-mail software you are using.

Bcc: This stands for **blind carbon copy**. A copy of the e-mail will be sent to that e-mail address, but none of the other recipients will be able to see that a copy has been sent. In this example, a copy has been sent to the representative at the sports centre – **Bcc** has been used instead of **Cc** because the sports centre representative does not want her e-mail address to be known by all the members of the club. Notice that this e-mail address does not appear anywhere in the received e-mail, shown below.

Attachments: Only text can be included in the main body of an e-mail, so if you want to e-mail other file types such as images and videos, you need to include them as attachments.

Attachments do not open automatically, you usually have to click on them to download them.

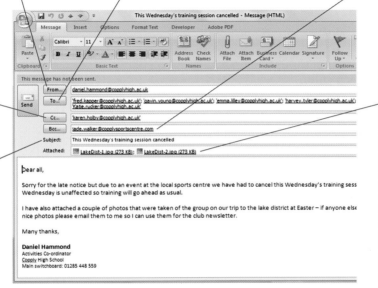

 Example of an e-mail

Reply: When you read an e-mail, you have the option to reply. Clicking reply will open a new, blank e-mail so that you can send a reply back to the e-mail address in the **From** field.

Clicking **Reply to All** will send an e-mail to all of the e-mail addresses in the **From**, **To** and **Cc** fields.

Forward: Clicking **Forward** will forward a copy of the e-mail to an address that you choose. You can also add comments to the e-mail before forwarding it.

 Example of the received e-mail

Managing the address book

All e-mail providers have an address book where you can store the e-mail addresses (and sometimes other contact information) of the people you e-mail. The advantage of this is that when you create an e-mail, you can just look up the person you are e-mailing in the address book and select their e-mail address instead of typing it in each time.

You can add new contacts to the address book, edit e-mail addresses of contacts whose details have changed and delete contacts that you are no longer in contact with.

Mailing lists

Look at the e-mail **To** field in the example in Screenshot **C** on page 75. There are several addresses here and it would be time consuming for the activities coordinator to type them all in every time he needed to contact the group. It would also be easy to make a typing error – just one wrong character would mean that someone would not receive the e-mail.

The activities coordinator runs several different clubs and regularly e-mails the members of each club.

To save time, the coordinator has created a mailing list for each club that contains the e-mail addresses of all the members in that club. When he needs to send an e-mail to a specific club, he just selects the mailing list he needs from the address book.

As members join and leave a club, the activities coordinator edits the mailing list by adding and deleting e-mail addresses.

E-mail storage

E-mails are like files, and they need to be organised into folders, stored and backed up just like word-processing or spreadsheet files.

When you receive an e-mail, it automatically goes into your inbox. The inbox is one of several folders that you will have in your e-mail account. Others are:

- **Sent items** – contains copies of all the e-mails you have sent.
- **Drafts** – contains all of the e-mails you have started to write but have not sent.
- **Outbox** – e-mails that are complete and are waiting to be sent. For example, if you are offline any e-mails you try to send will remain in the outbox. When you are online, these will be sent, and a copy will be put in the sent items folder.
- **Junk mail** (sometimes called spam) – contains all e-mails that either the ISP or virus checker thinks are junk/spam.
- **Deleted items** – contains e-mails you have recently deleted. This folder is usually emptied automatically so do not expect an e-mail that you deleted a week ago to still be there!

As well as the folders above, you can create more folders in order to organise your e-mails. For example, the activities coordinator might create the folders shown in Screenshot **E** to help him organise his e-mails.

Boost your grade!

E-mail signature

An e-mail signature is a block of text (and sometimes a small image) that appears at the end of every e-mail you write. Once you have set it up, it will appear automatically in each e-mail you write, although you can choose to delete it. It is useful if you always want your name and contact details to appear on each e-mail as it saves you typing it in every time.

Did you know ??????

There are all sorts of rules about the way you should write e-mails, such as not writing in capital letters and always including the original message in your reply. For more information on this, try typing 'e-mail etiquette' into a search engine.

AQA Examiner's tip

You will probably already know how to send and receive e-mails, but for the exam you need to be familiar with all of the features of e-mail software mentioned in this section, some of which you may not have used before. Make sure you know what each feature is used for and practise using them in your own e-mail account.

```
⊟ 📁 Mailbox - Daniel Hammond
   ⊟ 📁 Activities emails
         📁 Duke of Edinburgh
         📁 Football 5-a-side
      ⊟ 📁 Rock climbing
            📁 Lake District trip
         📁 Squash league
   📁 Drafts
   📁 Inbox
   📁 Junk mail
   📁 Outbox
   📁 Personal
   📁 Sent items
```

E *E-mails organised into folders*

Junk mail, spam and spam filters

Junk mail, also known as spam, is mail that is sent in bulk to users who have not requested or opted in to that e-mail list. It is frequently sent by companies trying to make money by advertising products or services, or from organisations trying to gather personal details or obtain money from you by illegal means.

Most e-mail providers and virus checkers will automatically scan your e-mails for spam and put suspicious messages straight into a junk mail or spam folder. This means that when you open your inbox you should not see messages that you do not want.

Spam filters work by blocking known spammers and looking for key words in messages. These rules are not entirely accurate and it is normal for some genuine e-mails to end up in your junk mail or spam folder. To prevent this, you can add a sender to a list of safe senders. You should also check your junk mail folder regularly to check for e-mails that have been put in there by mistake. You should never reply to a spam e-mail, even to ask to be removed from the list. If you do, the spammers know your e-mail address is real and live, so they will use it even more.

■ Instant messaging

When you send an e-mail, you do not know whether the recipient is online, so do not know when your e-mail might be read or when they will reply. However, with **instant messaging** you know that the recipient is online before you begin, and that what you type will appear on their screen as soon as you click Send. Instant messaging allows two or more people to have a conversation in real time.

Activity 5.1

Organising your e-mails using folders

If your inbox contains hundreds of e-mails, some dating back over a year, then you almost certainly are not organising your e-mails properly! Sort your e-mails into about five categories and create a folder for each. Go through the e-mails in your inbox and decide if they should remain there, be deleted, or filed in one of the folders you have created.

Did you know ??????

A report published in 2007 found that 94 per cent of all e-mails sent during the previous month were spam. Companies questioned said that spam was their biggest ICT problem.

Did you know ??????

Examples of online providers of instant messaging are Skype, Facebook, Gmail and MSN Messenger.

Summary questions

1. When using a search engine, which search terms would you use if you wanted to find the following?
   a Ingredients for salsa sauce, but with no entries relating to salsa dance lessons.
   b The name of the artist who sings the track 'Other side of the world'.
   c Information on hotels or hostels in Oxford.

2. a What is the difference between the e-mail address fields marked Cc and Bcc when you send an e-mail?
   b Suggest one reason why you might use each type of field.

3. How is instant messaging different from e-mail?

4. Name two folders other than the inbox which are usually found in an e-mail account. Give a brief description of which e-mails are stored in the folders you have named.

Web logs (blogs)

Web logs (usually shortened to 'blogs') are a type of website where people post comments on a particular subject. There are a few different types of blog, including:

- **Personal blogs** – these are used as a sort of online diary. For example, an amateur racing driver who writes (or 'posts') details of each race and track day complete with photos and videos for friends and family to view and to post comments.

- **Corporate blogs** –web pages containing updates on what a company has been doing, which might include recent events or forthcoming store openings. A company may use this to keep customers updated and also to find out customers' opinions by looking at the comments being posted by visitors to the blog.

- **News and views** – blogs created to update people with news on a specific topic. For example, the BBC has a blog on climate change where relevant findings and news items are posted. People can subscribe to the blog to be kept up to date with new entries, and readers can also post comments on each blog post.

- **Micro blogs** – Twitter is an example of a micro blog, where users write very short updates (about 140 characters) on what they are doing (known as 'tweets'). This results in a blog made up of many short entries that can look like a running commentary of someone's life. Twitter allows people to subscribe to other people's tweets. This means that you can keep up to date with the movements of friends and family, or your favourite personalities, by subscribing to their tweets.

Key terms

Web logs: usually abbreviated to blogs. These are websites where people or organisations write entries about recent events or on a particular subject.

links

If you are not familiar with Twitter, go to **http://twitter.com** and have a look.

The BBC has a large selection of blogs on various subjects. Look at some of the blogs available on their website at **www.bbc.co.uk/blogs**. On the same page you will also find more information about blogs in general, including some FAQs.

AQA Examiner's tip

You should be familiar with what web logs (blogs) are used for. Look up some examples of blogs created by individuals as well as companies – it will help you in the exam if you can remember some real-life examples.

A blog will always display the most recent entry at the top of the page, and the date of the blog entry is always clearly marked.

Blog posts can contain photos within the text. This photo is hyperlinked to a larger version of the article for people to read.

People are invited to comment on each blog post. You can read the comments by clicking on the **Comments** hyperlink.

Other fun features can be used in blogs, such as a vote as seen here – visitors to the blog just click to vote.

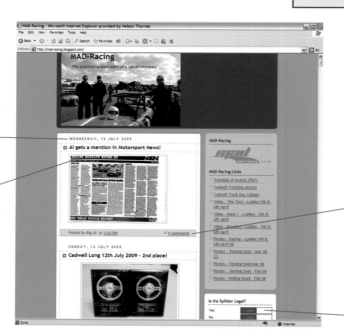

F *Example of a blog*

Social networking sites (k!)

A **social networking** website is a website where individuals and organisations each have a profile page and can link to other individuals and organisations. The links might be based on friendship, common interest or similar background (such as going to the same school). Some popular examples of social networking websites that you will probably already be familiar with are Facebook, Bebo and MySpace.

Using a social networking site

Before you can begin using a social networking site, you have to create a profile for yourself. Your online profile is made up of one or more web pages containing information about you. Your profile might include personal information, such as the name of the town where you live or the school that you go to, details about your interests, and photos or videos you have taken or that you like. Companies and clubs can also create a profile, which might contain information such as contact details and photos of recent events.

Linking with other people

Once you have an online profile, you can link to other people or companies who also have a profile. You can find them on the social networking site by searching for them by name or using information you know about them that they may have included in their profile, such as the town where they live or the school they attend. On some social networking websites every user has a unique user name, so you can find someone by typing in their user name if you know it.

Communicating with other people in your network

People to whom you have linked become part of your network. You can talk to people in your network by:

- sending them a message (just as you would send an e-mail) – which they can read when they log on to their page on the networking site
- instant messaging – many social networking sites provide instant messaging. You can see who is currently logged on to the networking website, and send a message that instantly appears on their screen
- sending status updates – you can write a sentence stating what you are doing, or just an opinion. This status update can be read by people in your network. People can also write comments on your profile that others can view.

Uploading files to your profile

You can upload photos and videos to your profile too. Sometimes you will have to download an additional piece of software known as a **plug-in** so that you can do this. It allows you to search your computer for the photo or video file and then upload it. You can also organise photos into albums and add a description to each one.

Dangers and risks of social networking sites 🔵k!

Writing personal information about yourself online can be risky and you should be aware of how this information might be used by someone who is not a friend. The risks of social networking sites are covered in more detail in Chapter 8, pages 112–113.

Privacy

You can select who can see information about you online by changing your privacy settings. For example, it is normal for individuals to set privacy settings so that only people they have links with (those who are part of their network) can view their personal profile.

Abusing social networking websites

Over the last few years there have been several cases where people have used social networking sites to pretend to be someone they are not. Examples include:

- creating an account under someone else's name, and posting information that might damage their reputation
- trying to connect to people who are not friends in order to view personal information on their profile and to use it in identity fraud.

Viruses and hacking

There have been many cases of people hacking into social networking sites and creating viruses. They often try to get sensitive personal information such as credit-card details. These usually work by asking you to download a file (or by directing you to another website which tries to install a file) which then infects your computer. The dangers of viruses and hacking are covered in more detail in Chapter 7, page 97.

Activity 5.2

What privacy options are there?

If you have a profile on an online networking website such as Facebook or Bebo, log in and look at the different privacy options. What is the most extreme setting you can choose to make your information available to the least number of people?

Activity 5.3

Identity fraud on social networking sites

Use a search engine to search for court cases involving social networking websites such as Facebook, where users have pretended to be someone they are not. There are a few high-profile cases involving celebrities that you may already be familiar with.

Case study

Facebook users hit by virus

Many viruses have been targeted at Facebook's 120 million users. Some are created just to cause minor issues and annoy users, but some viruses are more serious and are designed to illegally collect information about users.

A virus called Koobface was designed to collect confidential information such as credit-card details. The virus was spread by sending a message to Facebook users that looked as if it was sent by a friend. The message said: 'You look funny in this video', or: 'You look just awesome in this new video'. The recipient of the message was then encouraged to click a link to view the video. When they clicked the link, a download of the latest version of Adobe Flash Player started, which was when the virus downloaded to the user's computer.

Once the Koobface virus had infected the computer, there were two ways that it obtained the person's credit-card details. The first was to wait until they bought something online, when it recorded the details that they typed in. The second way was to search the computer for details that had already been entered and saved from previous online purchases.

Forums

An Internet **forum** is an online discussion website where users can post comments in an open conversation. Typically forums are created for people to discuss particular areas of common interest. Some examples of forums are:

- car enthusiasts' site where members discuss the relative merits of new or classic cars
- software developers' website where people can post queries about the software and the developers can post solutions
- forum on a news website where people can post opinions about the featured news article.

Podcasts

A **podcast** is a file that you can download from the Internet to play back on a portable audio player or computer.

Podcasts are used for a variety of purposes. They are mainly used for content that changes or is updated frequently, such as:

- Education: learning a language, downloading university lectures.
- Business: marketing and promotion of products, staff training videos.
- Recreation: radio shows, music playlists.

Podcasts can be audio or audio and video. Some examples of podcasts are as follows.

Audio only:

- Radio 1 Chart Show: a bite-sized run-down of Radio 1's weekly Official Chart Show top 40.
- Coffee Break Spanish: a weekly 20-minute Spanish lesson.

Audio and video:

- Sky Sports Boots 'N' All: weekly highlights of Rugby League
- NASA Cast Video: daily news and features from NASA's missions.

Podcasts versus normal music and video downloads

The important difference between podcasts and other downloads is that podcasts are normally part of a series made available for download on a regular basis, often daily or weekly. Software (such as Apple iTunes) can detect when a new podcast in a series you like is available, and automatically download it. You select which podcasts to download by subscribing. There are hundreds of free podcasts as well as some that you have to pay for.

Activity 5.4

Forums

Look at the website http:// news.bbc.co.uk/cbbcnews/ hichat. There are many forums here – called message boards – on different topics ranging from TV series to current news items. Choose a forum to see what sort of thing people are writing, and find out how you would add your own comments.

G *An MP3 player can be used to listen to podcasts*

Making your own podcast

It is possible for anyone to create their own podcast and make it available for others to download using the Internet.

The basic steps you need to take to make your own podcast are:

- Record your podcast using a digital sound recorder, and load it onto a computer.
- Upload the recording to an online server in MP3 format.
- Create an online blog that includes a podcast feed.
- Subscribe to your podcast.

There are websites that make it easy for you to create a podcast. You just create an online account, then provided your computer has a microphone the website will lead you through recording, uploading and making your podcast available for download. Have a look at Odeo: **www.odeo.com.**

Summary questions

1 For each of the following situations, suggest either a web log, forum or social networking site:

a Ellie is going travelling in her gap year and wants to upload frequent updates and photos to a web page so that friends and family can see where she is and what she is doing.

b David has formed a film club that meets once a week to watch a film. He would like a way for all members of the club to discuss online which films they would like to view at the next screening.

c Chirag is about to take his A Levels and move away to university. He would like an easy way to keep in touch with his school friends as well as new people he meets.

2 On a social networking site, how would you use privacy settings to reduce the risk of someone accessing personal information about you?

3 Mark each of these statements as true or false:

a A podcast has sound only, not video.

b People can subscribe to a podcast.

c A podcast is usually part of a series.

d You need a portable media player such as an iPod to be able to listen to a podcast.

In this chapter you will have learnt:

✔ which features are found in web browser software

✔ how to send and receive e-mail, as well as manage e-mail folders and the address book

✔ how to send and receive e-mail, control who an e-mail is sent to and include attachments

✔ how to manage an e-mail address book and organise e-mails into folders

✔ what a search engine is and which search terms to use to get relevant results

✔ what a web log (blog) and forum is, and how they are used by individuals and organisations

✔ what social networking sites are, how to use them and how to manage the risks associated with them

✔ what a podcast is and how it differs from a normal music or video download.

AQA Examination-style questions

1   A search engine is
   A   hardware used to help find information on the Internet.
   B   software used to find information on the Internet.
   C   hardware used to send e-mails.
   D   software used to send e-mails.
   (1 mark)
   AQA, June 2007

2   An increasing number of people use e-mail (electronic mail) as a method of communication. For many of these people it is gradually replacing other means of communication such as fax, telephone and post.
   (a) Explain what is meant by the term *e-mail*.   *(1 mark)*
   (b) i   Which of the following is an **advantage** of using e-mail compared to using **post**?
          A   The e-mail will usually arrive quicker than the post.
          B   The e-mail can be sent worldwide.
          C   The e-mail can contain pictures.   *(1 mark)*
       ii   Give **one** other advantage of using e-mail compared to using post.   *(1 mark)*
       iii   Give **one** disadvantage of using e-mail compared to using post.   *(1 mark)*
   AQA, June 2007

3   An increasing number of people are writing their own web logs (blogs).
   (a) Which **one** of the following is a well-known blog website?
          A   E-book
          B   Blog4U
          C   Twitter
          D   YouTwit   *(1 mark)*
   (b) Describe what is meant by the term *web log*.   *(2 marks)*
   (c) Give **two** reasons why web logs are becoming increasingly popular.   *(2 marks)*
   (d) Give **two** possible disadvantages to the visitor of using social networking sites when at work.   *(2 marks)*
   (e) Discuss the advantages of using a web log compared to using a social networking website.   *(3 marks)*

4   An increasing number of people are joining social networking sites.
   (a) Which **one** of the following is a well-known social networking website?
          A   E-book
          B   Face-to-face
          C   Facebook
          D   Netbook   *(1 mark)*
   (b) Describe what is meant by the term *social networking*.   *(2 marks)*
   (c) Give **two** reasons why social networking websites are becoming increasingly popular.   *(2 marks)*
   (d) Give **two** possible disadvantages to the visitor of using social networking sites.   *(2 marks)*
   (e) Discuss the advantages of using a social networking website compared to using a web log (blog).   *(5 marks)*

6.1 Data logging

Data logging is the process of collecting data over a period of time. There are many situations where data logging is used both in the home and in industry, for example monitoring the temperature of an office or a greenhouse.

Data is collected using sensors. Sensors feed data into a computer, the computer stores and processes the results, and sometimes an action is taken depending on the data values detected.

Data logging can be done manually, but in industry it is usually done by computers. Computers can access locations that a human cannot, and they can read data many times faster. This means that data can be logged using computers in situations where it was not previously possible.

Types of sensor

Sensors are used to detect physical quantities, for example heat, sound, temperature and pressure. A variety of different types of sensor are used depending on what sort of physical quantity you are trying to log. Think about the sorts of sensors that might be found in your home:

- a heat sensor (called a thermistor) used by the central heating to keep the temperature within a set range
- a movement sensor or infrared heat sensor for a burglar alarm to detect people inside a room.

Objectives

Become familiar with the different types of sensor available, and how they are used for data logging.

Understand the advantages and disadvantages of using computerised data logging.

Be familiar with how to write simple commands in control software to give instructions to a robot or device.

Know all of the stages of the control-feedback loop, and be able to identify how this is used in real-life systems.

Activity 6.1

Identifying sensors

Sensors are used in many devices all around us. Look around your classroom or your school. Try and find devices that use sensors – examples include security alarms and temperature controls. Write a list of all the sensors you find, what it is that the sensor is detecting, and where you found it.

A *Thermostat and infrared heat sensors*

AQA Examiner's tip

You need to be aware of the different types of sensors available. You should be able to recommend a type of sensor for a given scenario. See the Appendix on pages 131–136 for a list of sensors and their uses.

The process of data logging 🔑

Data logging always takes place over a period of time. The data from each sensor is recorded at set time intervals.

Data logging does not always involve computers – it can be done manually. You have probably done some manual data logging in science class, for example heating a beaker of water to boiling point then measuring the temperature every 20 seconds for five minutes as it cools. In that example, the **logging period** is five minutes and the **logging interval** is 20 seconds.

At the other extreme, scientists monitoring climate change might take a daily reading of carbon dioxide levels in the atmosphere over many years. In this case the logging period is years and the logging interval is one day.

Advantages of computerised data logging 🔑

Although data logging can be done manually in many situations, there are several reasons why you would use computerised data logging instead.

Computers can:

- run 24 hours a day, 365 days a year and are cheaper than employing someone to do the same thing
- take very accurate and consistent readings – they eliminate human error in taking readings
- take readings with very small logging intervals – for example, a computer could take a temperature reading hundreds of times per second
- be placed in locations that are not accessible to humans, or are dangerous or hazardous – for example inside a volcano or on Mars
- immediately analyse the data and take action if required – for example switching on a heater or sounding an alarm
- automatically present the readings as graphs or tables
- log data from many sensors at the same time.

There are also disadvantages of automatic data logging, such as:

- buying and setting up the automatic logging can be expensive
- faulty sensors may not be noticed immediately, resulting in incorrect readings
- if the equipment fails, new readings will not be taken and existing data may be lost.

> **Key terms**
>
> **Logging period:** the total length of time that data is being recorded.
>
> **Logging interval:** the length of time between recording each measurement.

> **AQA Examiner's tip**
>
> Learn the terms logging period and logging interval. The period is always longer than the interval.

> **Remember**
>
> Make sure you understand the advantages and disadvantages listed. It is a good idea to memorise at least two advantages and disadvantages for the exam, and give examples of each.

Automatic data logging in food transport

Automatic data logging is frequently used in the food industry to log the temperature of food whilst it is in transit. By law, companies who transport food have to show proof that the temperature of the food has been kept at a specified level. In order to do this, food transport companies install data loggers in vehicles that remotely log the temperature and transmit the readings back to the company headquarters.

In this case, using automatic data logging enables companies to keep track of the temperatures without involving the driver. This removes the possibility of human error with temperature reading, and also makes it impossible for the drivers to submit false results.

Case study

Automatic data logging in racing

Data loggers are used by both amateur and professional race teams. The data logger is fixed to the race car and can either transmit the results in real time back to the team, or can log the data for download later to a PC.

These data loggers measure quantities such as:

- Location, using a GPS sensor. This enables the team to locate exactly where the car is on the track, from which they can calculate current speed, lap times, and 'split' times (time to complete a specific section of a lap).

- Acceleration using an accelerometer. This measures forward acceleration and deceleration through braking. It also measures the sideways g-force experienced by the driver and the car as it goes around corners.

All of these results help the driver to understand the different forces on the car, and where lap times can be improved. It would be impossible for the driver to measure those quantities and log them – especially whilst driving! A data logger that can transmit the results in real time to a race team enables the team to give immediate advice to the driver about how to make the car go faster.

B *Formula 1 race teams receive essential information from the cars using data loggers*

Did you know ??????

Sensors need to be calibrated before they can be used. This checks their accuracy to be able to measure the changes taking place. Calibration matches against a known scale.

Summary questions

1 Below is a list of situations where data logging is used. Match each situation to one of the following logging intervals:

- half a second
- five seconds
- one hour
- one day.

Give a reason why you have chosen these intervals:

a A temperature sensor in an office building that is part of the air conditioning system. The system switches the air conditioning on or off to keep the temperature within a preset range.

b A pressure sensor on an aeroplane that monitors cabin pressure. If the pressure falls below a certain value oxygen masks are automatically released.

c A sensor measuring pollen levels in central London. The results are fed back to news stations to include in a morning update for hay-fever sufferers.

d A humidity sensor in a plant pot that is part of an automatic plant watering system.

2 A patient is in hospital and is attached to a heart-rate monitor. A screen displays the heart rate as a graph and as a number of beats per minute. List five reasons why an automated system is used to do this instead of a nurse manually taking a pulse.

3 For each of the systems below, suggest which one of these sensors will be used:

- movement sensor
- light sensor
- pressure sensor
- contact sensor

a A security light that switches on when you walk near it.

b A computer game with a dance mat that senses when you jump on a specific area of the mat.

c A fridge light that switches on when you open the fridge door.

6.2   Control software

Control software is used to make robots and other devices move around remotely or act automatically. Control software is a type of applications software used to write instructions. These instructions can be simple directions such as 'move forward one square', or they might be more complex such as 'if the temperature falls below 20 degrees, switch on the heater'.

You are surrounded by control software. It is what makes the burglar alarm sound if a window sensor is broken, and it makes the shop door slide open automatically when you walk up to it. Electronic gadgets and toys also operate using control software.

Key terms

Control software: software used to programme robots and devices with instructions so that they can act remotely or automatically.

Turtle: a small robot, either real or on-screen. Simple instructions are used to programme it to move around.

Case study

How are traffic lights controlled?

Traffic lights are an example of a system that uses control software. Some use external sensors and some run on a fixed timer.

The simplest system switches the lights in a fixed sequence at fixed times. The times are set according to historical data collected about traffic flow. The traffic-light system does not monitor the current state of the traffic. The timing of the lights will not change as a result of current traffic conditions. This system is fine for fairly quiet junctions without heavy traffic flow, but for busy junctions a more sophisticated system is used.

The second type of traffic-light system uses sensors to detect current traffic movements. There are magnetic sensors located under the tarmac at junctions that detect the movement of vehicles passing over them. All of the traffic data is transmitted back to a central computer. Using information collected from all of the sensors, the central computer calculates the optimal timing sequence for the traffic lights. This information is then transmitted back to the lights, so that the timing is constantly adjusted according to real-time traffic conditions.

C   *Traffic lights*

The turtle *k!*

This section focuses on control systems that do not use external inputs or sensors. Control software can be used to give a list of instructions either to an on-screen robot or a real-life robot – often called a **turtle**. You can write instructions that tell it to move around the screen in a specific pattern.

Here you will look at how to write a simple list of instructions to make a turtle pen move around a grid in a chosen pattern. The pen will then sketch a diagram.

The instructions to make the pen move are:

- **UP:** lifts the pen up
- **DOWN:** puts the pen down on the paper
- **FORWARD 1:** moves the pen forwards one square on the grid
- **BACK 1:** moves the pen backwards one square on the grid
- **LEFT:** moves the pen one square to the left on the grid
- **RIGHT:** moves the pen one square to the right on the grid.

Did you know ?????

Examples of control software are StarLogo and Flowol. StarLogo allows you to write simple instructions. Flowol is more advanced and you can write more complex instructions using flow charts.

Using these instructions, if you wanted the pen to draw a simple square in which each side was the length of two grid squares, the outcome would look like this (assuming that the pen starts in the UP position).

It is good practice to add an UP instruction at the end to return the pen to the up position where it started.

Activity 6.2

Using different instructions

The instructions used will vary depending on which software you are using. More importantly, the instructions in the exam will probably be different to those you have used before! But the good news is that each instruction that you use in the exam will be explained in the same way that the instructions have been explained in Diagram **D**.

Using the following list of instructions, write down how you would make the pen draw the same square as the one in Diagram **D**.

- PU: Pen Up – raises the drawing pen so that it stops drawing
- PD: Pen Down – lowers the drawing pen so that it starts drawing
- FD 1: Move forwards one square
- BK 2: Move backwards two squares
- RT 90: Turn right through 90 degrees
- LT 90: Turn left through 90 degrees.

Now use the instructions given here to write your initials, even your name. You will have to style some of the letters; C, B, O and K are some examples of letters that will be difficult to draw using the turtle. It is possible though – use some squared paper to help you.

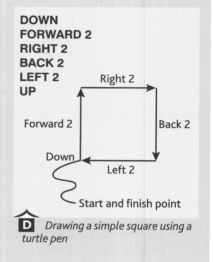

DOWN
FORWARD 2
RIGHT 2
BACK 2
LEFT 2
UP

D *Drawing a simple square using a turtle pen*

Using control software to programme a water-jet cutter

Case study

Most machines and robots used in industry are programmed using control software. Examples include robots that spot-weld car body parts together and industrial milling and lathing machines.

Water-jet cutters are used in industry to cut complicated shapes from sheets of metal, glass or plastic, using a very high-powered thin jet of water. They are very powerful and can cut precise and intricate shapes.

The path of the water jet is programmed using control software. The control software used to write the instructions for the water-jet cutter will have many built-in sections of code and rules to help the programmer. For example, if the programmer enters the type of material and the thickness, the control software can advise what the maximum speed of the cutter can be and there will be no risk of the jet failing to cut right through the material. It can also automatically calculate a suitable acceleration, deceleration and speed for corners without causing any distortions.

A simulation of the water jet path will be shown on screen before the cut is actually made. This enables the programmer to correct any errors in the code, and to refine the path or speed up the cutter as required.

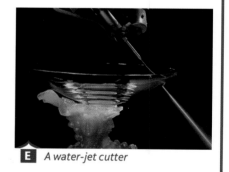

E *A water-jet cutter*

Control software used in computer games

All computer games are programmed using control software, including those that you play on a PC or on a dedicated games console such as an Xbox, PlayStation or Nintendo.

The programming involved uses the same concept as the simple examples above using the turtle – but it is a lot more complicated!

Take the example of a car race game. The turtle is replaced with an on-screen car, most likely a three-dimensional car with very sophisticated graphics. The control program is not a set of pre-written instructions; instead the instructions are given in real time by the person playing the game.

Of course, when you are racing a car in a computer game, you are not typing out line-by-line directions for the car! Instructions for the car are usually input either through simple keystrokes or using a joystick, games controller or steering wheel. The control software then converts these inputs into programming code that changes the position of the car on the screen.

There will be many more aspects involved in a computer game – the control software developed for the latest games will take a team of programmers months to write. There are many different parts of programming code that control other aspects of the game, including the speed of the car, the movements of other cars in the race, and the constantly changing background scenery.

Control-feedback loop

In the control software example of the turtle pen, the robot turtle is told to move without first reading an input from a sensor. In many control systems, the robot or device must receive an input from a sensor before taking an action. In those systems, there is a control-feedback loop.

There are three main stages involved in the control-feedback loop: input, processing and output. Take an example of a temperature-controlled greenhouse:

- The **input** to the system is the current temperature of the greenhouse, taken from sensors.
- The input is then **processed**. The current temperature is compared against set values. These values are saved as storage in the memory of the system. The current temperature is also recorded and stored for later analysis.
- The **output** is to switch the greenhouse heaters either on or off (or leave them as they are) in order to keep the temperature within the desired range.

This output affects the input because the heater being turned on or off will affect the current greenhouse temperature. This is the system **feedback**.

> **Key terms**
>
> Feedback: the way the output influences the input. For example, a heater switching on will affect the temperature input.

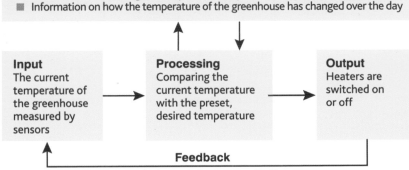

Storage
- Information on the range of temperatures required in the greenhouse should be
- Information on how the temperature of the greenhouse has changed over the day

Input	Processing	Output
The current temperature of the greenhouse measured by sensors	Comparing the current temperature with the preset, desired temperature	Heaters are switched on or off

Feedback
Heater being switched on or off affects
the temperature of the greenhouse

F *An example of a control-feedback loop to control greenhouse temperature*

> **AQA Examiner's tip**
>
> Learn the stages of the control-feedback loop:
>
> - input a new value
> - respond to it by processing (for example turn on heating)
> - check reading, if not as required then change the input value (feedback).

The autopilot control-feedback loop

Aeroplane autopilot systems were originally introduced to control the aircraft during long flights to allow the pilot to rest. Today, autopilots are very complicated systems that can fly a plane even without a pilot. Many autopilot systems can actually perform better than a human pilot. They can make a flight smoother, and can perform landings in zero visibility.

The autopilot works by collecting information about the current position and status of the plane using many sensors. The human pilot sets the course for the plane to travel. The autopilot compares the two sets of information. The autopilot then makes adjustments to the aeroplane to keep it on course. In order to do this, the autopilot uses the control-feedback loop.

Look at each part of the system.

The system inputs are:

■ readings from various sensors, such as speed, acceleration, wind speed, location, altitude and angle of the plane in two directions (wing to wing and front to back)

■ the desired speed, altitude, location and route, etc. as set by the human pilot.

The system outputs are:

■ signals sent to three sets of motors on the aircraft:
   - elevators: devices on the tail of the aeroplane that control the pitch of the plane – the angle of the plane front to back
   - the rudder: also on the tail of the plane, the rudder controls how the aircraft twists right or left
   - ailerons: these are the flaps on the wings that move up or down to control the roll of the aircraft; this is what tilts the plane left or right, making one wing higher or lower than the other.

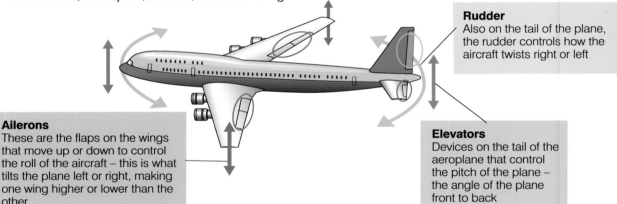

Ailerons
These are the flaps on the wings that move up or down to control the roll of the aircraft – this is what tilts the plane left or right, making one wing higher or lower than the other

Rudder
Also on the tail of the plane, the rudder controls how the aircraft twists right or left

Elevators
Devices on the tail of the aeroplane that control the pitch of the plane – the angle of the plane front to back

G *Autopilot control-feedback loop*

Processing

The autopilot system is constantly monitoring the status of the plane and comparing it to the desired status.

Look at just one part of the autopilot system, the control-feedback loop involving the pitch of the plane.

Storage
A data logger (called a flight data recorder or 'black box recorder') constantly records and stores the status of the aircraft and the inputs from the sensors. This is used to analyse flight safety and engine performance, as well as what went wrong in the event of an accident. Information is also transmitted back to local air traffic control centres so that they can track the location and status of the aircraft.

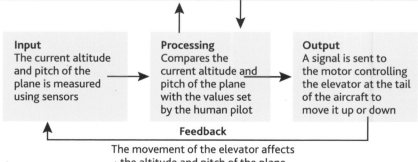

Input	Processing	Output
The current altitude and pitch of the plane is measured using sensors	Compares the current altitude and pitch of the plane with the values set by the human pilot	A signal is sent to the motor controlling the elevator at the tail of the aircraft to move it up or down

Feedback
The movement of the elevator affects the altitude and pitch of the plane

H *Feedback loop to control the pitch of a plane*

The advantages of autopilot over a human pilot are that the autopilot can monitor the input from many sensors and process them instantly and many times per second. This means that it can respond to very small changes, very quickly, resulting in fast response times and a smoother flight.

Of course, autopilot systems can and do fail, although fortunately this is rare. All aircraft have a simple override switch, where the pilots can switch off the autopilot system and control the aircraft manually if they believe it is not functioning correctly.

Activities 6.3

The control-feedback loop in household appliances

Consider the following two kitchen appliances:

- a cordless kettle that boils water then switches off as soon as the water temperature reaches 100 °C
- a toaster, which when the slot is pushed down, will toast the bread for 3.5 minutes then pop it up.

1 Which one of the appliances uses a control-feedback loop?

2 What type of sensor is needed for that control-feedback loop?

3 Draw a simple diagram with brief explanations of the control-feedback loop for that system. Your diagram should include the INPUT, PROCESSING, STORAGE and OUTPUT stages.

4 Choose one other household appliance and repeat steps 2 and 3 using your chosen appliance.

Summary questions

1 This list of instructions (right) is used to make an on-screen turtle create the shape shown.

a What do the FORW and RIGHT instructions do?

There is another instruction called REPT that does the following: REPT 3 [ ]: It repeats the instructions contained in square brackets [ ] three times.

b Write how you would use the REPT instruction to create the triangle shape above using fewer lines of code.

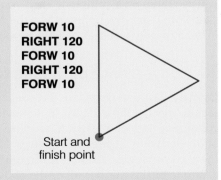

FORW 10
RIGHT 120
FORW 10
RIGHT 120
FORW 10

Start and finish point

2 A race car has a spoiler that changes its angle automatically to give a constant downforce regardless of speed, wind and air temperature. Label the following parts of the system as INPUT, PROCESSING, OUTPUT, STORAGE and FEEDBACK:

a a pressure sensor measures the current downforce on the spoiler

b the spoiler angle is adjusted

c the current downforce is compared against desired downforce

d the new spoiler angle affects current downforce

e the current downforce is logged for later analysis.

6.3 Mobile technologies

Today there are many different types of device that allow you to access the Internet – not just desktop computers!

There are various technologies and pieces of hardware that make this possible, such as:

1 **Laptops** (also known as notebook computers): these work in the same way as a desktop computer, but they are much smaller. They come in different sizes and weights, but they all tend to have a small keyboard with a fold-down flat screen.

2 **Smart mobile phones** (also called smart phones, PDAs (personal digital assistants) or palmtops): these are mobile phones that offer many of the features found on a computer. Some of the features you will find on most smart phones are:
   - Internet access
   - e-mail that automatically downloads to the phone when it is received
   - a calendar and contacts address book
   - applications software such as word processing and spreadsheets
   - large memory for storing data, and the option to insert additional memory cards
   - a digital camera.

WAP

Wireless Application Protocol (WAP) is a technology that enables mobile-phone users to view specially adapted websites on their phone screens. If you have a mobile phone with access to the Internet, and the websites you view look simplified and have a different layout from when you see them on a computer, then you are probably looking at a WAP site. Note that newer phones like the Apple iPhone do not use WAP, and instead display websites exactly as you would see them on a computer.

Convergence of mobile technologies

Over the last few years, we have seen many different types of technology combined into single devices. It used to be that your computer, phone, television, satellite navigation system and electronic organiser were all separate devices. Now, it is common to find all these technologies (and more) in one package. An Apple iPhone is an example of this – it has all of the above features and more packed into a small handheld device.

Satellite navigation systems

Satellite navigation systems are often used by drivers to find their way around. They use the global positioning system (GPS), which has 24 satellites named NAVSTAR orbiting 18,000 km (11,000 miles) above earth. The receiver listens for signals from these satellites. If it can pick up signals from three or four different satellites, it can calculate your

I Apple iPhone

J Satellite navigation or 'satnav' display

precise location. It can then plot a route for you to follow. Satellite navigation systems use touch screens to make it easy for the driver to use on the move. They also give voice commands so that the driver does not have to look at the screen while driving.

Activity 6.4

Look up five different mobile digital devices on the Internet. A good place to start would be a website selling mobile phones.

Draw a table like the one below. Look up details on each device and fill in the table. Which one would you buy and why?

Device name	Portability – is it small enough to fit in a pocket?	Performance – is it powerful enough to run a variety of applications, such as Pocket Excel?	Storage/ memory – how much memory does the device come with? Is it possible to expand the memory?	Connectivity – for example, does it have 3G, Wi-Fi or Bluetooth?	Applications – what sort of applications are available to use on the device?

Summary questions

Identify which device would be most suitable for each of the following situations. Give reasons for your choice.

1　Sara is taking a three-hour train journey from her office to a conference where she will be giving a short presentation. She has prepared most of the presentation but intends to make some final changes on the journey.

2　Raul is an area manager for a restaurant chain and is spending the day travelling around different restaurant locations. He needs to be in contact with head office and to view his e-mails at all times. He also needs to update his calendar and address book regularly.

In this chapter you will have learnt:

✔　the variety of sensors used to measure physical quantities such as heat, light and pressure

✔　how data logging is used, and what is meant by logging period and logging interval

✔　the advantages and disadvantages of using computerised data logging

✔　what control software is used for, and how to write simple instructions for robots and devices using control software

✔　the different stages of the control-feedback loop and how to identify these stages in real systems

✔　the advantages of mobile technology.

AQA Examination-style questions 🔴

1   The definitions below are all related to data logging and control systems. From the list
     given below, choose the term that best matches the definition.

A	actuator	B	calibrate	C	data logging
D	encryption	E	feedback	F	graphing
G	keyboard	H	logging interval	I	modem
J	period of logging	K	sensor	L	wizard

     (a) Collecting and storing of data at regular, fixed intervals over a period of time.   *(1 mark)*
     (b) An input device used to measure environmental conditions.   *(1 mark)*
     (c) The time taken between one reading and the next.   *(1 mark)*
     (d) To compare readings of a sensor against those of a known scale.   *(1 mark)*

AQA, June 2008

2   A group of pupils from a school enter a competition to build a programmable robot.
     The robot must move around an obstacle course without bumping into the walls. The
     walls are shown in black in the diagram below.

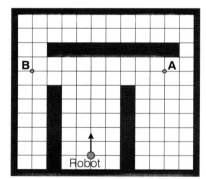

     Examples of the instructions needed to programme the robot are given below.

Instruction list	Movement by the robot
Fd2	Moves the robot forwards two squares
Bk2	Moves the robot backwards two squares
Rt90	Turns the robot right through 90 degrees

Command list
Fd4
Fd5
Fd6
Rt90
Bk4
Bk5

(a) Using **only** the commands from the Command list above, write down instructions to move the robot from the starting position shown to point A. *(2 marks)*

(b) Again using only the commands from the Command list, write down instructions to move the robot from the original starting position shown to point A, then to point B and finally back to the original starting position. *(3 marks)*

AQA, June 2008

3   A home central heating system uses a monitoring and feedback system to control the temperature of each room in the house.

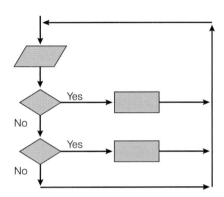

(a) The system is used to maintain the temperature of the living room at 23°C. Copy and complete the flowchart to show how this system works by writing a letter for each answer in the flowchart boxes.

A	Turn off the heating	B	Turn on the heating
C	Disconnect the heating	D	Read the temperature in the room
E	Is the temperature greater than 23°C?	F	Is the temperature less than 23°C?
G	Is the temperature equal to 23°C?	H	Print the temperature of the room *(3 marks)*

(b) What device would be needed to read the temperature in the room? *(1 mark)*

(c) Why might the central heating system need such a device in each room? *(1 mark)*

AQA, June 2007

4   A weather station is located on the seafront of a large seaside town.

(a) Name **one** sensor that could be used to take the temperature. *(1 mark)*

(b) What is the name given to this automatic process of collecting and recording data at fixed intervals? *(1 mark)*

(c) Give **one** advantage of the weather station using more than one sensor to record the temperature. *(1 mark)*

(d) Give **two** advantages to the weather station of collecting data automatically rather than by hand. *(2 marks)*

(e) Each sensor used by the weather station has to be calibrated to a known scale before it is used. Explain why this is important. *(2 marks)*

AQA, June 2006

7.1 Legal issues relating to the use of ICT

ICT plays such an important part in modern life that it has many implications for the way society operates. It affects the way that businesses are run and the things that people do in their leisure time. ICT can have an impact on the environment and on everyone's privacy. This means that laws are needed to control the way ICT is used.

■ The Data Protection Act 1998

From the moment we are born, data about each of us is collected and stored by many organisations. The **Data Protection Act 1998** (DPA 1998) is designed to protect the privacy of people about whom data is held. These people are known as **data subjects**. Organisations that hold personal data are called **data users**. In the UK, the Data Protection Act 1998 is enforced by the **Information Commissioner**.

Data users have to register with the Information Commissioner and state what data they hold, what they intend to use it for and how long they intend to keep it stored. They also have to agree to follow the rules of the DPA 1998, which are known as the eight data protection principles. These say that data must be:

- fairly and lawfully processed
- processed for limited purposes
- adequate, relevant and not excessive
- accurate and up to date
- not kept for longer than is necessary
- processed in line with your rights
- secure
- not transferred to other countries without adequate protection.

The rules sound complicated, but most of them are really common sense. Data users must make sure that they follow the rules when they collect data. If they intend to pass your data on to anyone else, they must ask your permission. They have to make sure that they keep their records up to date and delete them when they are no longer needed. They must make sure that only authorised people can access the data. Each organisation holding data must appoint a **data controller** – a person who is responsible for making sure the organisation follows the rules.

Your rights

As a data subject you have the right to:

- see what data is being held about you and ask the organisation holding your data to provide a copy of it. The organisation can make a small charge for sending it

Objectives

Know how the Data Protection Act 1998, Computer Misuse Act 1990 and Copyright and Patents Act 1988 affect the use of ICT.

Understand how plagiarism and illegal downloading of material affects society.

Understand the effects of ICT on the social and economic aspects of life.

Understand the political, ethical and environmental issues affecting the way ICT is used.

AQA Examiner's tip

Make sure you know the difference between a data user (for example your school) and a data subject (for example you). The Act applies to personal data.

Key terms

Data Protection Act 1998: a law designed to protect the privacy of personal information.

Data subjects: people about whom data is stored.

Data users: people or organisations that store personal data.

Information Commissioner: the government department that enforces the Data Protection Act 1998.

Data controller: the person in an organisation who is responsible for ensuring the Data Protection Act 1998 rules are followed.

- have anything corrected that is inaccurate
- ask the organisation not to process information if it might cause you damage or distress
- refuse to have your data used for direct marketing (sometimes called junk mail)
- complain to the Information Commissioner if you think a data controller has broken the rules
- claim compensation through the courts if you have been caused damage by a data controller breaking the rules.

Exemption

There are some cases where the DPA 1998 does not apply. These are called **exemptions** to the Act. There are a large number of these, but some of the most important ones are:

- where national security may be put at risk
- where information must be available to the public
- where information is for personal use within families
- where information is needed to prevent and detect crime
- where information is needed to collect taxes.

◼ Keeping data safe

It is important for data users to keep your data safe. It is also important that you protect your own system against computer **viruses**. Viruses are pieces of computer code that can delete or corrupt data files. They are often sent as e-mail attachments or web links. Some viruses affect the user's instant messaging package. They send virus-infected files to the contacts in the user's address book. If you think an attachment or message looks suspicious do not open it.

It is also possible to corrupt computer data, either deliberately or accidentally. It is important to follow the rules about how and where files should be saved. There is more information about version control in Chapter 9, page 127.

The rules of sensible behaviour should also be applied when contributing to Wikis. Adding content that may not be correct might confuse other people. For that reason, you should also be careful to check the reliability of any information that you use from such sites.

Computer Misuse Act 1990

The Computer Misuse Act 1990 sets out to prevent unauthorised access to computer data. Accessing a computer system that you are not authorised to use is sometimes called **hacking**. You might think that hacking is done by people outside an organisation, but that is not entirely true. Most networks allow users to access limited parts of the system. If a user tries to access a part of the network that they are not authorised to use, they are breaking the Computer Misuse Act 1990.

The Computer Misuse Act 1990 has three levels of offence:

- Level 1: accessing a computer system, software or data that you know you are not authorised to use.

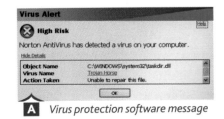

A *Virus protection software message*

- Level 2: unauthorised access with the intent to commit a further offence such as fraud or theft.
- Level 3: unauthorised modification of computer material. This could mean changing or deleting data or planting a virus.

The person committing the offence does not actually have to benefit from what they do. Level 1 of the Act would apply to someone who used another person's password just to have a look at various parts of the system. The important point is that they know they are not authorised to see those parts of the network. This would be a level 1 offence.

An example of a level 2 offence would be someone who used their unauthorised access to find out someone else's Internet banking password.

Creating a virus and deliberately sending it to another computer would be a level 3 offence.

■ Copyright and Patents Act 1988 🅺

Copyright legislation is designed to protect **intellectual property**. It applies to books and music as well as computer software and images. Material that is protected by copyright has a © symbol next to it, and that means that it cannot be used or reproduced without permission.

Copyright legislation also applies to computer software. If you buy a computer package, you are actually buying a licence to use it. A **software licence** lays down the rules that you have to agree to if you want to use the software. The licence agreement is usually displayed at the beginning of the installation procedure and you have to click to say you agree to it before you install the software.

> **Example**
> Imagine that you have a brilliant idea for a new computer game. You spend a lot of time planning and working on your idea, you pay people to draw it and write the programming code and you are ready to carry out a huge launch so that people can buy it. On the day before your launch is due, you find that someone else has stolen your code and published the game at half the price you can afford to sell it for. You would not be very happy, would you? The game was your idea, which makes it your intellectual property. If you had applied for copyright, the other person would not be able to use your code without your permission.

Types of software licence

- A single-user licence will allow you to install and use the software on one computer. Sometimes it will allow you to install the software on your laptop too, as long as you never use both copies at the same time.
- A multi-user licence will state how many copies of the software you are allowed to install. Businesses will use multi-user licences when they install software that runs across their network.
- Site licences apply to some educational software packages. They allow the school to install as many copies as they want, but only within that school.
- Shareware software is usually available on a free trial to begin with. Sometimes the trial version only works for a limited period of time

∞ links

The BCS (British Computer Society) has developed a Personal Data Guardianship Code which is at **www.bcs.org**.

Key terms

Intellectual property: ideas or creations such as software or music that can be protected by copyright.

Software licence: a legal agreement stating how a piece of software may be installed and used.

Did you know ??????

Breaking the Computer Misuse Act 1990 is punishable by a prison sentence of up to five years.

AQA Examiner's tip

Learn **two facts** about the Copyright and Patents Act 1988. The easier ones to remember are:

- It **prevents** the theft of your ideas (called 'intellectual property').
- It applies to computer software/music/video/books.

or has some functions removed. For example, you may not be able to save the files you create. If you like the software, you then pay for it and the restrictions are removed.

- Public domain software is sometimes called freeware. You can install and use it without having to pay for it.

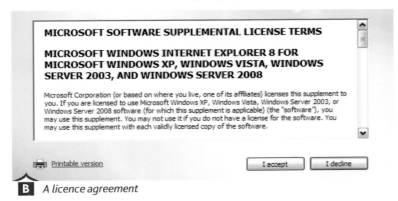

MICROSOFT SOFTWARE SUPPLEMENTAL LICENSE TERMS

MICROSOFT WINDOWS INTERNET EXPLORER 8 FOR MICROSOFT WINDOWS XP, WINDOWS VISTA, WINDOWS SERVER 2003, AND WINDOWS SERVER 2008

Microsoft Corporation (or based on where you live, one of its affiliates) licenses this supplement to you. If you are licensed to use Microsoft Windows XP, Windows Vista, Windows Server 2003, or Windows Server 2008 software (for which this supplement is applicable) (the "software"), you may use this supplement. You may not use it if you do not have a license for the software. You may use this supplement with each validly licensed copy of the software.

Printable version   [I accept]   [I decline]

B *A licence agreement*

Plagiarism and copyright

With so much content available on the Internet, it is very easy to obtain information. It is also easy to cut and paste that information into your own work. If you mark that information as a quote from another source, then that is acceptable. If you simply use it without saying where you got it from, that is **plagiarism**, which is a form of cheating.

The Internet is a useful place to carry out research, but it is important to write about what you find in your own words. You should only select the parts of the material that are important, and you should always quote your sources so that you can prove you have not cheated.

Some images and other material may be subject to **copyright**. This means you are not allowed to use them without permission. This material will be marked with a © symbol. It is not enough to crop an image to remove the symbol – you should ask permission to use it or choose another image.

> ### Key terms
>
> **Plagiarism:** copying a piece of writing, music or other intellectual property from someone else and presenting it as your own work.
>
> **Copyright:** a legal right given to someone who creates documents, pictures or music. It means that other people cannot use that work without the permission of the copyright owner.

University applications

Students applying for places at British universities do so through an organisation called UCAS. As part of that process, they have to write a personal statement that tells the universities about themselves. It is important that the personal statement is written by the student in their own words.

In 2007, UCAS estimated that about 5 per cent of applicants copied parts of their personal statement from the Internet or from other students. UCAS is unhappy about this as a personal statement should be the student's own work.

UCAS needed a system to stop this plagiarism. They used detection software called Copycatch. It compares every application with thousands of personal statements posted on websites as well as those from previous years.

If three sentences or more (about 10 per cent of the statement) appear to have been copied, the forms are passed to UCAS staff to be looked at in more detail.

UCAS reported that:

'Almost 800 medical applications had personal statements containing phrases directly borrowed from three online example statements. Some elements of sentences were found to be remarkably common:

- 370 contained a statement starting with: "...a fascination for how the human body works..."
- 234 contained a statement relating a dramatic incident involving "...burning a hole in pyjamas at age eight..."
- 175 contained a statement which involved " ...an elderly or infirm grandfather...".

Data taken from the UCAS website (www.ucas.ac.uk).

Case study

Music downloads

It is perfectly legal to upload to a website such as MySpace music that you have composed and recorded, so that other people can listen to it and download it. If you want to stop people using it without your permission, you have to apply for copyright.

Music bought and sold commercially is subject to copyright. If you buy a CD or music through a digital download, you are buying the right to play it for your own personal use. You do not have permission to pass it on to other people, even if you do not charge any money for doing so.

It is illegal to upload music bought commercially onto a **peer-to-peer site** that allows other people to download it. If you download music illegally, the artist and music company, which paid a lot of money to produce it, do not get paid for the work they have done.

The music industry takes illegal downloading of music very seriously. They have prosecuted individual people who have uploaded or downloaded music illegally. Some ISPs will also warn users and close their Internet account if they continue to download illegal content.

The same arguments apply to illegally downloaded video.

Did you know ??????

The British Phonographic Industry (BPI) is a trade organisation that aims to protect and advance the British music Industry. It has prosecuted people for illegal downloads. For example, the parents of teenagers who did not understand that the downloads were illegal have been prosecuted. In 2005 the mother of a 14-year-old was fined £2,500 for this offence.

Summary questions

1. What law would you be breaking if you did the following?

   a Downloaded the new album of your favourite singer and gave copies to all your friends.

   b Printed out a customer's finance record and left it on your desk when you went home.

   c Used a computer that a member of staff had accidentally forgotten to log off, and you looked at another student's personal file.

2. James wanted to buy a new computer on interest-free credit, but the shop said his credit rating was not good enough. James is worried because he does not owe money to anybody.

   a What rights does James have under the Data Protection Act 1998?

   b What would you advise him to do?

   c James has just moved house. Why do you think this could have caused the problem?

∞ links

Creative Commons is a non-profit organisation that encourages creators of music and video to share it with other people. It provides a method of licensing that allows creators to control what their content can be used for. Find out more about Creative Commons at **http://creativecommons.org**.

7.2 Social and economic issues relating to the use of ICT

Changing pattern of commerce and industry due to increased use of ICT

ICT in industry

Developments in ICT have had huge impacts on the way that businesses are run. In manufacturing industries, computer control is often used to design and produce products. The designer can use **CAD** (computer-aided design) to draw a product on screen. The data from the design is then fed to the machine that will produce it. This is called **CAM** (computer-aided manufacture).

Robotic arms can be used to move goods on automated production lines. The progress of goods can be tracked as they are manufactured. The stock level of components used in the production process can be monitored and items can be re-ordered automatically when they fall below a minimum level. This ensures that the correct amount of stock is always available.

The effects on products and people

These developments have had an effect on the products themselves and the jobs of the people who make them. Products have tended to become more standardised. This is because it is expensive to set up a production line. So it is more cost effective to make large amounts of one product rather than smaller amounts of two or three variations.

Fewer workers are needed on automated production lines, so many jobs have been de-skilled. Watching a machine produce things does not take the same sort of skill as producing the things yourself. On the other hand, the design and setting up of the production run is a very skilled job.

It is important to remember that some products will never be suitable for automated manufacture and that many people still value handmade goods because they can be a little bit different.

ICT in commerce

Commerce, the way people buy and sell things, has changed too. **E-commerce**, or electronic commerce, has grown massively in recent years. Most high street shops also have an e-commerce website and many retailers, such as the bookseller Amazon, do not have shops at all. This reduces the company's costs as they only need warehouse premises, which tend to be cheaper to rent than high street stores.

E-commerce is convenient for shoppers as they can choose and buy products from home rather than travelling to the shops. This saves time and money. It is also easier to shop around for the cheapest price online. Disabled people find online shopping particularly useful.

On the other hand, there are delivery charges to pay and you do need to be at home when the goods are delivered. It is not possible to see

> **Key terms**
>
> **CAD**: computer-aided design. Uses a computer to produce drawings of the design of a product. It may also be used for automatic calculation of weights, strengths, etc.
>
> **CAM**: computer-assisted manufacture. Often uses output from CAD packages. It uses computers to control the tools that manufacture or assemble products.
>
> **E-commerce**: uses the Internet for commercial tasks such as selling goods or services.

C *Example of CAD used to design a housing development*

D *Automated production line*

the quality of goods or try them on, so there is a danger that you will be disappointed when they arrive. It is also important to choose a reliable supplier, otherwise the goods may not arrive at all!

It is now possible to order goods from virtually anywhere in the world. That also causes problems as some goods such as weapons and prescription drugs are legal in some countries and not in others.

■ Changing pattern of employment due to increased use of ICT

ICT has changed the way that many businesses operate. Manufacturing processes that used to be done by hand are now often performed by computer. This can change the way a business operates, closing down some types of business and creating new ones. In many cases the number of people needed has been reduced, and the jobs that they do have changed. Many factories have become smaller but, with a much higher level of technology, they need powerful computer networks and clean operating environments.

UK newspaper industry

For a long time the English newspaper industry was based in Fleet Street in central London. The newsprint was set by skilled operators on huge typesetting machines. In the 1970s and 1980s, things began to change. Rupert Murdoch and Robert Maxwell became heavily involved and the decision was made to move newspaper printing out of the centre of London.

The layout and printing of newspapers at the new sites were computer controlled and needed a different type of skill. The manual skills of the print workers were no longer needed. This caused the workers to strike. In 1978 strikes meant that *The Times* and *The Sunday Times* were not published for 11 months. The old methods were inefficient and expensive. Some of the newspapers retrained their existing workers, some simply sacked them.

Newspapers are now laid out by computer and can be sent anywhere in the world to be printed. This means that holidaymakers in Spain can see their favourite newspaper almost as quickly as they would in the UK.

Use of the Internet and growth of 24-hour news channels present new challenges to the newspaper industry. Most newspapers also have online editions and some are struggling to compete for the advertising income that pays for their production. Some newspapers have gone out of business because of this.

Teleworking

Powerful computer networks have meant that more people are able to work from home through a process known as teleworking. They log on to the company network via their own computer and work mostly from home, perhaps visiting the office from time to time for meetings. This way of working suits some people, particularly those with disabilities or those who care for children or elderly parents.

Working from home reduces the time and money that is spent travelling to work, and the reduction in traffic is good for the environment. A wider range of employment may be available if you do not have to live near the place that you work. Businesses need less office space, thus reducing their costs. On the other hand, teleworkers miss out on the social side of work. There is a danger that home workers may feel isolated and less able to discuss work problems than those in a shared working environment. It may also be difficult to avoid distractions when working from home. This could be anything from watching TV to friends visiting during working hours. Teleworkers must set aside time each day when they can concentrate on work.

E   *A teleworker*

Example

The increasing use of computers and networks has made it possible for people to work in a less traditional way. A bank's financial adviser used to visit clients and discuss their requirements. They would write them down and then work on them on a computer in the office.

Now the financial adviser can find information about clients' products (insurance policies, mortgages, etc.) and accounts over the Internet. They can access the bank's computer system using a security-encrypted laptop. They can work from home rather than going into the office. E-mail can be accessed via mobile phone and details of appointments sent by text messages.

The result of this technology is that working hours become more flexible, as people do not have to be in the office at set times. When they do go into the office, it operates a 'hot desking' system. That means no one has their own desk, they just use whichever one happens to be free. For many people, this more flexible way of working will increase their job satisfaction.

■ Social and personal effects of ICT

ICT has changed the way that many people communicate. Twenty years ago, social communication was done in person or over a land-line telephone. Today, most people in the UK have a mobile phone and access to the Internet. These have widened the choice of methods that people use to keep in touch with each other. Personal websites and blogs can be set up to let the world know what you are up to. Instant messaging makes it possible to chat to a friend whilst working on a computer. The biggest development in recent years has been social networking sites such as Facebook, MySpace and Bebo as well as blogs such as Twitter. There are even junior versions of these sites, such as Club Penguin.

Many media celebrities use social networking sites as a way of keeping their profile in the public eye. Politicians use these sites to put over their message. It is now much easier for old friends to keep in touch. Most of us would not write dozens of letters about our personal news. Social networking allows us to tell others about the events in our lives, from the trivial to the really important.

On the other hand, these sites can create pressure. Having 300 friends listed on a social networking site is unlikely to mean you have 300 friends in reality. The pressure amongst some teenagers to have a lot of friends listed means that they accept people onto their site that they do not actually know. Personal safety online is covered in more detail in Chapter 8.

> **Boost your grade!**
>
> **Monitoring in work**
>
> Computer-based work allows managers to monitor employees extremely closely. Take call centres, for example. Every call that is made can be recorded, so every word that the employee speaks in a day can be recalled and discussed. This may be used for training or to deal with customer complaints.
>
> The number of calls processed can be calculated. Employees may be rewarded for efficiency or disciplined for a poor call rate. This can cause some employees to become stressed.

> **Did you know** **?????**
>
> Many celebrities and politicians use Twitter. In 2009 the Times Online published a list of famous Tweeters, listed in order of how many people had signed up for their posts. Stephen Fry came top of their list, which also included pop star Britney Spears and former American Vice-President Al Gore.
>
> 'You can lead a celeb to twitter but you can't always make them tweet.'
>
> http://technology.timesonline.co.uk/tol/news/tech_and_web/article5641893.ece

The growth in personal communication methods means that many people find it much more difficult to relax and get away from the pressures of daily life. A busy business person used to go on holiday and forget about everything for a week or two. Now it is very easy for their colleagues to phone or e-mail about the slightest problem, meaning that the break is much less of a holiday than it used to be.

On the other hand, people with restricted mobility or those who are shy about communicating in person, can feel much more able to connect with others using electronic methods.

Equality of computer access and ICT skills

Computer skills have also become very important in the employment market. Businesses tend to look at computer skills when choosing employees, and the UK government has listed ICT along with English and maths as a basic skill that all students need.

In the UK, the Computers for Pupils scheme aims to help some of the most disadvantaged secondary-school children. It aims to improve their education and life skills by putting a computer into the home. Local authorities identified as having eligible schools and pupils in their area have been given funding to buy ICT equipment.

Outside the UK, students in developing countries may not have access to a computer – they may not even have access to an electricity supply on which to run one. This puts them at a disadvantage compared with students in wealthier countries. The One Laptop per Child scheme is researching ways of providing computer access to children in developing counties.

Accessibility

It is important that computers are made as accessible as possible for people with a range of disabilities. People with visual impairment often find computers extremely useful once they have made some adjustments to the display. The operating system can change the zoom settings to make the screen display bigger, although this means the user will have to scroll around more. Changing the colours of the background and text can make it much easier for some people to see. Websites can be set so that they read out the text and descriptions of the pictures. Scan-and-speak systems can scan paper documents and read them out loud. This means that a visually handicapped person can deal with their own letters rather than needing someone else to read them.

Specialised input devices such as eye-tracking devices or a mouse that can be operated with your foot can help physically handicapped people to become more independent.

∞ links

http://industry.becta.org.uk/display.cfm?resID=20615 describes the Computers for Pupils scheme.

http://laptop.org describes the One Laptop per Child scheme.

F *This eye-tracking device uses infrared beams and cameras to allow the user to control the computer with eye movements*

Summary questions

1 'Computers steal people's jobs and cause redundancies.' Do you agree with this statement? Draw a mind map or list to help you focus your ideas on computers and employment. Draw up a table of advantages and disadvantages of computers in business and industry.

2 'If computers are important in education, what happens to children who do not have access to them?' Discuss this statement, explaining some of the schemes that are available to provide computer access to children at home and abroad.

7.3 Political, ethical and environmental issues relating to the use of ICT

National databases

The DNA database

The UK police keep a national DNA database. DNA samples obtained for analysis from the collection of DNA at crime scenes and from samples taken from individuals in police custody can be held in the national DNA database. One aspect of this that is unpopular with many people is that the DNA of people who are questioned but not charged with a crime has been stored on the database.

There is no doubt that DNA analysis has helped the police to solve many crimes, and some people believe that it would be better if everyone had their DNA stored. Others believe it is a breach of human rights. The European Court of Human Rights has ruled that the storage of DNA from innocent people is illegal. This may stop it being collected or it may just place a time limit on how long it can be stored.

National identity cards 🄺

In some countries around the world, citizens are expected to hold an identity card. These are used as proof of identity, for example if they wish to open a bank account. In some countries they are compulsory, in others they are voluntary. In 2008 the UK government launched its identity card scheme. The cards will be compulsory for foreign nationals living in the UK and voluntary for UK citizens.

The cards use biometric data from faces and fingerprints to identify individual people. The government believes that the ID cards will improve national security. They are compulsory for key workers at airports, as the government believes this reduces the chances of terrorist attacks. The cards cost £30 each, and many people feel that this charge is unfair and a waste of taxpayers' money. Others feel that it is an invasion of privacy.

Security and privacy 🄺

Storing data on a large scale always causes concerns about the privacy and security of the data. Several cases of data loss from government systems have been reported. The fear of identity theft makes people very anxious about personal details falling into the hands of criminals. Some personal data gathered for one purpose could easily be used for a very different one. If data from the NHS Connecting for Health database became available to private companies, people with a risk of future health problems might be unable to get insurance or find a job.

∞ links

NHS Connecting for Health is one of the largest schemes of its kind in the world. It aims, amongst other things, to store all patient data centrally. Find out more about it at **www.connectingforhealth.nhs.uk.**

∞ links

The National Policing Improvement Agency website **www.npia.police. uk** gives more information about how the police use technology to help them solve crimes.

> **Did you know** ??????
>
> The UK's DNA database is the largest of any country. Approximately 5.2 per cent of the UK population is on the database compared with 0.5 per cent in the USA. The database has expanded significantly over recent years. By the end of 2005 more than 3.4 million DNA profiles of known active offenders were held on the database.

> **Activity 7.2**
>
> **Identity cards – what do you think?**
>
> Information about identity cards is on the Directgov site: **www. direct.gov.uk**. Follow the link to Government, citizens and rights. Search for information on the identity card within this website.
>
> Then search for articles on identity cards on the BBC news website (**www.bbc.co.uk**). These will reveal some other facts and opinions.
>
> Write a short article about the identity cards, explaining your opinion on such matters as whether they should be compulsory and whether people should expect to pay for them.

The surveillance society

CCTV (closed-circuit television) is increasingly being installed as a crime prevention measure. Modern cameras can be operated remotely and produce high-resolution colour pictures. CCTV has been developed that is capable of recognising individual car number plates and recording them on central databases. The congestion-charging scheme introduced in London in 2003 uses this system. Facial recognition can also be used with CCTV footage and it has been used to identify criminals and football hooligans.

Many people worry that constant recording takes away their privacy. Others feel that if CCTV stops criminals, the loss of privacy is a price worth paying. It is unclear to what extent CCTV actually reduces crime. One report showed that CCTV reduced crime by 5 per cent, whereas over the same period, improving street lighting reduced crime by 20 per cent.

CCTV is not the only way that people can be 'spied on'. At the moment, MI5 can apply for a warrant that allows them to monitor phone calls, e-mail and web browsing. Government ministers are considering spending up to £12 billion on a database to monitor and store the Internet browsing habits, e-mail and telephone records of every person in Britain.

The government believe this is necessary in order to fight crime and terrorism. There are huge concerns about this idea on the grounds of privacy and security. Many government ministers are also very concerned about the cost and whether it is ethical to intercept private communications.

Using ICT to monitor the environment

ICT has the ability to store and process huge amounts of data very quickly. This makes it ideal for collecting data about weather and climate. Monitoring the environment can help to explain what is happening to the world's climate. It can also help to predict events such as floods, earthquakes, hurricanes and tornadoes. This makes it easier to prepare for natural disasters.

Oceans

NASA has sponsored a project called Estimating the Circulation and Climate of the Ocean. Phase II (ECCO2) is modelling global ocean currents, changes in temperature and salt levels in sea water, and the growth and melting of sea-ice in the polar regions.

It collects data from all available NASA satellites and from on-site instruments. It uses this data to produce images and models of ocean depth and sea ice. The changes in these images are then compared over a period of time. The images will help scientists to analyse the role of oceans in the climate, and the changes in the oceans in polar regions.

G *Nasa's QuikScat satellite measures winds over the ocean surface*

Case study

■ Sustainability and recycling

In recent years it has become clear that it is very important to manage resources such as energy and raw materials. Computers are used to design energy-efficient buildings and also to monitor and control their energy use. Monitoring systems can observe and control the consumption of gas, electricity and water. They can show organisations where they are wasting resources. They can also control the systems, for example by automatically turning off heating systems when offices are closed.

■ Impact of ICT on different populations

ICT has had a huge impact on many different communities and cultures. It has made it easier for people all over the world to communicate and trade with each other. The Internet has also made it much easier for people to find out what is happening in other parts of the world.

Until quite recently it was reasonably easy for governments to have some control over what people in their country knew. In wartime, they issued propaganda – carefully selected communications that told people about the war. The information was not always accurate, and could be biased to give people an impression, for example, that the war was going better than it actually was. This would be much harder now, as information and videos are sent back from war zones very quickly.

Some governments still try to control the access to information in their country.

In this chapter you will have learnt:

- ✔ how the Data Protection Act 1998 affects individuals and companies
- ✔ the importance of the Computer Misuse Act 1990
- ✔ about copyright law and how it protects against plagiarism
- ✔ the effect that ICT use has on employment
- ✔ the social impact of ICT
- ✔ how ICT has affected surveillance and security
- ✔ how ICT is used to monitor the environment, our natural resources and recycling.

Smart bins

Case study

Several councils are currently trialling the use of smart bins that monitor the amount of rubbish people throw away. They have a microchip embedded in them that weighs the amount of rubbish and charges the household accordingly.

∞ links

Optimal Monitoring (**www. optimalcomms.net**) is a company offering energy monitoring. Its website includes many case studies.

Summary questions ✓

1 **a** What does the term 'surveillance society' mean?

b Discuss the use of CCTV in Britain, explaining its benefits and drawbacks.

2 'The Internet must allow free speech for everyone.' Do you agree with this statement or do you think that the Internet should have some form of censorship? Explain your views in a short essay.

AQA Examination-style questions

1. Quickcallz is a high street company that sells a range of mobile phones. They are going to produce a leaflet that will contain text and clip art, to advertise their 'Summer Sale'. The owners of the shop are worried about the copyright on the clip art they are planning to use.

   (a) What is meant by the term *copyright*? *(1 mark)*

   (b) Which **one** of the following applied to the copyright clip art?

   A   Clip art is always free of copyright

   B   Clip art is never free of copyright

   C   Clip art is sometimes free of copyright *(1 mark)*

   (c) Give one penalty the owners could face if they broke the copyright law. *(1 mark)*

   AQA, June 2008

2. Give **four** responsibilities placed on **data users** by the 1998 Data Protection Act. *(4 marks)*

   AQA, June 2008

3. (a) National identity cards are considered to be a way in which the government could 'spy' on the general public. List **two** other ways in which this could happen. *(2 marks)*

   (b) Many people are concerned about the security of public data held by the government on laptop computers. Which **two** of the following would be the **most** suitable security measures to prevent their concerns?

   A   Ensure that government laptops have a lock.

   B   Ensure that all data on government laptops is encrypted.

   C   Ensure that government employees don't use laptops.

   D   Ensure that personal data is not stored on government laptops.

   E   Ensure that government laptops have a strong password with a combination of letters, numbers and symbols. *(2 marks)*

4. Which of the following ICT methods will help to monitor the environment?

   A   A computerised model of the UK

   B   A series of sensors placed throughout the UK

   C   An ICT-controlled recycling plant

   D   The use of low-energy wind turbines. *(1 mark)*

5. An increasing number of companies store vast amounts of information on their computer systems. Information is stored on a wide range of items such as details of their employees, customers and suppliers. It is vital that the information stored is accurate.

   (a) Describe the possible consequences to a company if some of this information is inaccurate. *(3 marks)*

   (b) Describe the ways in which the information stored by the company on the computer system may become inaccurate. *(3 marks)*

   (c) Describe the ways in which a company could reduce the risks of inaccurate data being stored on their computer system. *(4 marks)*

   AQA, June 2008

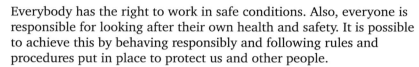

8 Using ICT responsibly

8.1 Health issues for computer users

Everybody has the right to work in safe conditions. Also, everyone is responsible for looking after their own health and safety. It is possible to achieve this by behaving responsibly and following rules and procedures put in place to protect us and other people.

Working with a computer all day can damage your health permanently if you do not follow procedures. People who use computers a lot often sit in the same position repeating the same physical actions over and over again. This can cause problems with their health. It is important to recognise those risks and try to reduce them as much as possible. Some health risks may be short term, such as a headache at the end of a busy day. Other risks, such as spinal damage, may be permanent.

■ Eye problems

Focusing on the screen for long periods of time can cause eye strain and headaches. This can be made worse if the screen is not clean or suffers from glare from reflected light. It is important to make sure that the lighting in the room is suitable and that you can adjust the screen brightness to a level that suits you. Computer users should have regular eye tests to make sure their eyes are healthy.

■ Wrist problems (RSI)

Using a mouse and keyboard over and over again can cause a condition called upper limb disorder. This is sometimes called **RSI** (repetitive strain injury). Symptoms include pain in the fingers and wrists and even in the shoulders. It is important that users make sure their wrists are in the correct position when using a keyboard. Some people find a wrist-rest helpful in reducing the symptoms of RSI.

■ Stress

All of us experience stress sometimes. Many jobs that people do can be stressful, and this is particularly true of some ICT jobs. In recent years, more and more people have been employed in call centres and data entry centres. In these jobs, the work that people do is monitored in great detail. Operators are expected to answer calls very quickly, and the calls are usually recorded in case of a complaint. If target call rates are set too high, operators may also be tempted to work through their breaks rather than fall behind. Some levels of stress are acceptable and necessary with important projects or exams. However, people must manage stress levels so that they do not put their health at risk.

Objectives

Understand the health issues that can affect people who use computers for most of their working day.

Understand some of the safety issues that can affect people working in office environments.

Understand the need to behave responsibly online.

Know how to prevent unauthorised access to data.

Did you know ??????

Some people suffer from a condition called photosensitive epilepsy. This means that flashing lights can bring on an epileptic seizure. You may have heard warnings given prior to some TV programmes. Flashing images on a computer screen can cause epilepsy too. Many computer games use these types of image, and it is very important not to play them for too long without a break.

Key terms

RSI: repetitive strain injury, a condition that causes painful joints in the wrist or fingers. It is sometimes called upper limb disorder. Using a computer for long periods of time can cause RSI.

Did you know ??????

Recent research suggests that RSI is more likely to be caused by overusing a mouse rather than overusing a keyboard.

Back and neck problems

Sitting in the same position for long periods of time can cause and aggravate back and neck problems. For that reason, it is very important to sit correctly when using a computer. You should take the following points into consideration:

- A well-designed adjustable chair will help to make sure your back is properly supported.
- Yours eyes should be level with the top of the monitor.
- Your feet should be resting comfortably on the floor or on a footrest.
- A monitor that tilts and swivels will also help you to find a comfortable working position.
- A well-designed workstation should have enough work surfaces for papers and other equipment to be arranged appropriately.

If your posture is not correct when you are sitting at a computer, you are in danger of developing back and neck problems and can even damage your spine permanently.

All of the above problems will also be helped by taking breaks or changing activity. Regular short breaks work better than one long break.

Health and safety at work

The risks discussed so far apply specifically to people who use computers for most of their working day. However, there are many more health and safety risks that apply to offices and other workplaces where computers are used.

Tripping

Many offices were designed for far fewer pieces of electrical equipment than are used today. This means that cables are sometimes run over long distances to reach power sockets. Even if cables are secured to the floor, it is still possible to trip over them. It is much safer to think carefully about where equipment is placed and have extra power sockets installed if they are needed.

Heat

Computers give off a lot of heat, and this can mean that rooms quickly become uncomfortably hot. Sometimes simple methods such as opening windows and using fans to circulate air may be enough to keep the room cool. The best way to maintain a comfortable temperature is to install air conditioning, although this is expensive and not particularly good for the environment. Switching computers off rather than leaving them on standby saves money and reduces the amount of heat given off. Server rooms need to be air conditioned as the equipment does not perform well if it gets too hot and may malfunction.

A *Good posture is extremely important when using a computer for long periods of time*

Electrical safety

All electrical equipment can become dangerous if it is not checked regularly for electrical safety, and computers are no exception. Users should get into the habit of looking at their computer equipment carefully and if cables or plugs become damaged they should report this. If equipment cannot be repaired safely it may need to be replaced. Electrical safety checks also reduce the risk of fire.

If the fire protection methods fail, suitable fire extinguishers need to be available. Fire extinguishers for electrical equipment must be filled with carbon dioxide. Carbon dioxide extinguishers have a black stripe on the bottle.

Computers can be damaged if their power supply fails. This can also cause the data stored on them to be lost or damaged. A **UPS** (uninterruptible power supply) contains a battery and can protect the computer by maintaining its power until the computer can be closed down safely. This is particularly important for servers. When the voltage of the electricity supply suddenly increases, this is called a surge. This can also damage equipment. A surge protector plug is a simple way to protect the computer from voltage surges. A UPS will usually have surge protection built in.

Hygiene

Like any piece of equipment, a computer should be kept clean. Food and drink should not be placed near to a computer. Keyboards are often used by many different people over the course of a day and all users should follow basic hygiene precautions. This includes washing their hands regularly, especially after coughing or sneezing. Specialist keyboard wipes will also help to keep the surfaces clean.

Lighting

The position of computer equipment should be planned carefully when the layout of an office is designed. Monitors should be positioned so that they do not suffer from the glare and reflection that can cause eye strain. Blinds can be fitted to windows to block out direct sunlight. Diffused lighting is less likely to cause glare and reflection than normal fluorescent tubes.

B *Carbon dioxide fire extinguisher*

Key terms

UPS: uninterruptible power supply. This protects a computer if the power fails by providing power until the computer can be closed down safely. It will also protect against voltage surges.

∞ links

www.hse.gov.uk/pubns/indg36.pdf is a leaflet published by the Health and Safety Executive that covers the health and safety aspects of working with computers.

AQA *Examiner's tip*

Learn four health risks. Start at the top of your body and work down:

■ Head – headaches – take a break.

■ Eyes – eye strain – eye tests/ adjust monitor distance/reduce screen glare/use diffused lighting.

■ Neck/back – neck/back ache – supportive adjustable chair/ monitor height position/use a footrest.

■ Wrists/fingers – RSI – use a wrist-rest.

Summary questions

1   Cassie uses a computer for most of her working day.

a   Give three health risks that using a computer this much may expose her to.

b   For each risk, suggest one thing Cassie can do to reduce the likelihood of it affecting her health.

2   Give two reasons why electrical equipment should have regular safety checks.

8.2 Responsible behaviour online

Staying safe and behaving responsibly 🎦

Using computer technology opens up exciting possibilities for interesting and creative work. It can also be lots of fun and help friends and family to keep in touch. As well as the right to use the technology, everyone is personally responsible for the way they use it.

You need to think about your conduct online:

- how you behave when you are online
- the material you view online
- the people you interact with online.

Keeping yourself safe

Social networking sites, instant messaging and chat rooms are all great ways to communicate. Online game sites allow users to chat when they play, which adds to the fun for a lot of people. Users create user names and use **avatar** characters to represent themselves online. In one way, this keeps people safe, because they are not giving out their real information. However, other users have to remember that they have no idea who the person behind the avatar really is. They can be of any age or gender and bear no resemblance to their avatar. It is easy to feel as if the people you chat with online are trustworthy friends, but the reality might be very different. For that reason, it is very important not to give out personal information such as an address or phone number or even your full name.

Page 125 in Chapter 9 explains how webcams can be used for videoconferencing. It is important to remember that webcams should only be used when talking to friends and family members. Never use a webcam to talk to someone you met online.

When you have been chatting to someone online, it is easy to feel that you know them well enough to meet in real life, but you need to think carefully about the possible consequences.

Arranging a real-life meeting with someone that you chat to online can be very dangerous. If you really feel you want to meet them, it is important to discuss the idea with your parents before making arrangements. You should also arrange to meet in a public place and take an adult with you. There are many documented cases of adults using the Internet to build up a young person's confidence. The adult gradually asks for photographs and contact details and finally asks to meet in person. This process, known as **grooming**, is a criminal offence, and has led to teenagers being assaulted and abused.

If you are a member of a group, you may receive e-mails that are sent to lots of people at once. You may even be responsible for sending out such e-mails to the group. These e-mails should be treated with care. If someone who receives the message then forwards it to another person, the e-mail addresses of everyone on the circulation list will also be forwarded. If you use the BCC (blind carbon copy) feature on your e-mail software, the people on your list will not see each other's e-mail addresses. It is important to respect other people's privacy in this way.

> **Key terms**
>
> **Avatar:** a picture that you choose to represent yourself online. It is safer than using a real picture of yourself.
>
> **Grooming:** a criminal offence where a person gradually builds up a young person's confidence online. They may then ask the young person to meet them in person.

C *An avatar is a picture or figure that you choose to represent yourself online. These are avatars from the 3-D virtual world* Second Life

Respecting others

It is easy to forget how many people can see a comment or photograph posted online, and how hard it is to take it back. In real life, at one time or another most people will say something that they later wish they had not. If they are brave enough, they will go to the person and apologise, and with any luck the apology will be accepted. If they made the original remark in front of other people, the situation becomes a little more difficult. If an unpleasant comment has been posted on a social networking site, then the situation is much worse.

> **Example**
>
> Emma and Sophie have been out together to a theme park. One of the rides made Emma feel unwell and Sophie took a video of her being sick, in which she looks awful. The video has been posted on Sophie's social networking page. All of Sophie's friends can see it, and so can all of Emma's friends. That means about 300 people have seen it so far. Emma is really upset and Sophie, who is not really unkind, immediately takes the video down. The problem is that one of Sophie's friends, who does not even know Emma, saved a copy of the video and passed it on to her friends. One of those thought it was really funny and posted it on YouTube. Suddenly, it has an audience of many thousands of people and it is totally out of Sophie's control.

Cyber bullying

Using text messages, e-mail and social networking to say things that are hurtful and upsetting is known as **cyber bullying**. In previous generations, once students went home from school they were in contact with only a few friends until the next day. With the availability of text messages, e-mail, mobile-phone calls, instant messaging and social networking sites, students can contact friends at any time of the day or night. If these methods are used for bullying, the person being bullied can feel that it is impossible to escape. Often this kind of bullying starts as a bit of a joke, but then lots of other people join in, and suddenly it is not funny any more. The other people may not do very much, but the person being bullied can feel isolated and insecure. There have even been cases where this kind of bullying has led to suicide attempts.

Things to remember

- If you are being bullied, tell someone. It could be an adult such as a parent or a teacher, or perhaps a peer mentor if your school has such a scheme.
- Cyber bullying leaves a trail of proof. Save text messages or instant messenger conversations. Take screenshots of websites. This proof makes it much easier to tackle the bullies.
- Remember that the bully is trying to look clever, funny or 'hard' to their friends. That means they are looking for a reaction. They want their victim to look foolish, unhappy or scared. If you do not react, they are not getting what they want, and so they will get bored and move on.
- Bullying is made possible because of people who join in. You may not have bullied that person, but you might have made it possible for someone else to do so because bullies need an audience.
- Do not just take the bullying – tell someone who can help!

Key terms

Cyber bullying: using computers and mobile phones in ways that make another person unhappy or uncomfortable.

links

The following links will give you more information about online safety.

Childnet International, a non-profit organisation working with others to 'help make the Internet a great and safe place for children', **www. childnet-int.org**. This Links page shows you lots of other websites where you can find out more.

Thinkuknow is a scheme run by the Child Exploitation and Online Protection (CEOP) Centre, **www. thinkuknow.co.uk**.

E-mails

Chain e-mails are often sent to lots of people. They sometimes contain jokes or even threats that something bad will happen if you do not forward the e-mail to lots of people. This passes all of the e-mail addresses already on the message to everyone it is sent to, and the number of e-mail addresses can become huge. If you do receive a chain letter, it is best to simply delete it. If the e-mail is in any way frightening, you should show it to an adult.

Flaming e-mails contain angry or abusive messages. They can sometimes happen, for example, if one user on a forum disagrees with another user. It is very easy to write something when you are angry and just press Send. An e-mail is sent immediately, and it is not possible to take it back. It is always best to give yourself time to calm down and think before reacting to anything that makes you angry.

Activity 8.2

Keep safe online!

Parents do not always understand the Internet particularly well. Produce a leaflet that gives the parent of a teenager information about why young people enjoy communicating online. It should also explain some of the hazards and how the parent can help keep their child safe.

Filtering content

Most schools and some home computers are set up with content-filtering software that restricts the material displayed. The rules will vary, but they will usually restrict access to 'hate' sites (websites that promote hatred, typically against people of a specific race, religion, or sexual orientation) and sites containing pornography, plus other sites that the school or parent feels are inappropriate. As sites get closed down, others open, and so even on filtered systems these sites may still be accessible from time to time. If you open an inappropriate site accidentally, you should immediately close it and tell a teacher or parent.

Some systems also filter e-mails, usually based on a list of forbidden words. The e-mails are sent to the system manager who then decides whether they should be passed on to the person they were addressed to.

Summary questions

1. 'Social networking sites are dangerous and should not be used by people under 16.' Do you agree with this statement? Explain the benefits of social networking for young people and also some of the hazards.

2. Most organisations reserve the right to read any e-mails sent using their system.
   a. Explain why they might choose to do this.
   b. Discuss whether you believe this is an invasion of personal privacy.

8.3   Preventing unauthorised access

Software methods

Firewalls

Anyone using a computer connected to the Internet should make sure they have a **firewall** in place as a defence against hacking. A firewall is a piece of hardware or software that prevents unauthorised access to a network or a specific computer. It limits the data that can be sent to and from the system, for example by blocking websites considered to be unsafe. Firewall software may also have intrusion detection built in. This will alert the user if anyone who is not using an authorised address attempts to access the computer.

User accounts and passwords

Most online systems are secured by way of **user names** and **passwords**, but some sites are much more secure than others. An online game site or bulletin board will not have high security levels. You should always assume that passwords on these sites may become visible to someone else. For that reason you should always use a different password on these sites to the password you might use for secure transactions. Sites such as Internet banking and reputable online shopping sites use **encryption** to protect their data. The **uniform resource locator (url)** of secure sites begin with https rather than the usual http, and they have a padlock symbol to show they are safe.

Networked computer systems allocate a user name and password to each user. You need that information to log on and it controls the rights that you have on the network. This may include the software you can use, the files you can see, and what access you have to files and directories. **Levels of access** are used to control what you are allowed to do to files, for example:

- **No access**: you cannot open the file and may not be able to see it at all.
- **Read only**: you can open the file and perhaps save a copy, but you cannot make any changes to the original file.
- **Read/write**: you can read the file and make changes to it, but you cannot delete it.
- **Full access**: you can do anything to the file, including deleting it.

> **Example**
>
> When you log on to your school network you may:
> - be allowed to use standard software packages but not the most advanced ones
> - have full control over your own user directory
> - have read-only rights to a common directory where you can access worksheets to use in class
> - be unable to see the teachers' directory
> - be unable to change the screen wallpaper or screensaver.
>
> All of these rights are controlled by your user name and password.

D *Padlock symbol*

Remember

A **PIN** (personal identification number) is an example of a number frequently used as a password, for example for a debit card or at an **ATM**. It is important to keep your PIN secret. As PIN stands for personal identification number, if you call it a PIN number, that would be a personal identification number number!

Most networks set rules that passwords have to follow. They may set a minimum number of characters or force the user to choose a password that has numbers as well as letters. The strongest passwords are the ones that are hardest to guess – lots of random characters with numbers, letters and other characters such as £ and $. They should also be changed frequently. The problem with setting rules such as these is that users then cannot remember their password and so they write it down.

Because user names and passwords control security, it is important to keep them secret and not share them with others. Your teacher cannot stop another student logging in as you and deleting your work if other people know your password. It may also mean that you get the blame for something you did not do, for example accessing inappropriate websites.

Biometric identification

Biometric methods use the characteristics of a person's body as a way of identifying them. Fingerprint recognition is available instead of a password on many laptops. Retina scanning, where a camera scans the back of a person's eye, is also used in some sophisticated systems. Voice recognition is also a form of biometric identification.

■ Physical methods *k!*

It is possible to prevent unauthorised access to computer systems using physical methods. The easiest way to do this is to lock and alarm the doors of the room that the computer is in. CCTV cameras can also be used to record images of people entering and leaving the room when it is unlocked. Choosing a room above ground level is also a good idea. The computers are less visible to potential thieves and it also makes it more difficult to carry the equipment away. Some security systems use voice recognition technology. The person wishing to enter the room speaks into a microphone and the system matches their voice pattern against stored data.

In high-risk situations it is also possible to clamp the computers to desks or install locks that prevent them being used. Workstations at which access to removable media drives is blocked prevent the unauthorised copying of data. This physically stops users copying data to USB sticks, CD-Rs, etc.

■ Keeping your money safe

Chip and PIN technology has made it harder for criminals to use stolen credit cards in high street shops. So criminals are now using the Internet to steal money. They use many different methods to trick people into giving their banking details, and these methods are called Internet fraud.

When you log in to a secure site such as those used for Internet banking, you sometimes have to enter some of the characters as well as your full password. Sometimes these are selected from a drop-down menu to avoid a criminal capturing the details through keystroke logging.

If you forget your login details, you can usually be reminded of them or allowed to change them. You will often be set security questions that you have to answer in order to identify yourself. These might include your date of birth or the name of your first school. Some websites use image code recognition to prevent people from creating lots of accounts automatically. The site displays a picture of some text and you have to type in the characters.

Phishing involves sending e-mails pretending to be from a bank, eBay or any other organisation that handles financial transactions. The e-mail says that the user needs to log on to a website and update their security details. This would give the criminal access to that person's account. The e-mails can sometimes look very convincing, but there are usually ways of spotting the fraud:

- Name. A genuine bank e-mail would always use a name, rather than 'Dear Customer'. The criminals do not know your name, so they cannot use it.
- The url (web address). The fraudsters will try to create a url that looks convincing, but they cannot use the bank's real url. These websites are sometimes called mirror-image websites, and they may look very realistic.
- The e-mail address that the e-mail came from. The criminal cannot use the bank's real e-mail address.
- Errors in spelling and grammar. Many of these e-mails come from abroad, and the English may not be correct.

The contact websites or e-mail addresses for these frauds are changed every few days, making the criminals more difficult to catch. A phishing filter can be used to scan the websites that you visit and alert you if they seem suspicious. The filter does this by comparing the website address against an up-to-date list of those known to be fraudulent phishing sites.

ATM fraud

ATM or hole-in-the-wall machines are the most popular way for most people to withdraw cash from their bank account. Another common fraud is to fix a device to the card slot that actually reads the details on the card. When the criminals collect the scanning device they have the information they need to produce a fake duplicate card and use it to withdraw money. You should look very carefully at any ATM you use.

Identity theft

Many people use the Internet for banking and shopping, and they set up an electronic identity for security purposes. This is made up of their name, address, user names, passwords and PINs. If a thief obtains this information they can steal money from bank accounts or buy goods online. This is called **identify theft** because the thief pretends to be the person online. Phishing e-mails try to get hold of this information, but they are not the only method used.

Some **spyware** looks for password files saved on your computer. Anti-spyware software can be set up to detect attempts to install spyware on your computer. Some operating systems offer to store passwords for sites that you use regularly. If this is a bulletin board or gaming site, that is not too much of a problem. If it is your Internet banking password, then it is a problem. For this reason, most Internet banking sites ask you to enter a selection of characters from your password and digits from your PIN rather than the whole thing.

E *Image code recognition*

Did you know ??????

Ebay, PayPal and the banks have e-mail addresses where these scams can be reported. If you are in any doubt as to whether an e-mail is genuine, forward it to the genuine organisation and ask them what to do. Do not click any website links or enter any personal information.

Did you know ??????

Some thieves go through the rubbish that people throw out, looking for information that might be used for identity theft. Remember to shred any paper with personal information on it before throwing it away.

Example

Phishing e-mails are not the only scams. Others involve telling people that they have won a prize in a lottery or draw that they have not actually entered. One famous e-mail that appears regularly tells the story of money in an account in a war-torn country. There is a large amount of money in a dead person's bank account that the writer cannot get out of the country. If you send your bank account details, they will give you half of the money. When you read the story, it is hard to imagine how anyone would believe it. It is true that not many people do, but it only takes one or two to make it worth sending thousands of e-mails. After all, e-mails cost very little to send.

▇ Acceptable use policies

Schools, colleges, businesses and other organisations usually have **acceptable use policies** in place that set out what users are permitted to do when using the organisation's computer facilities. They will include what websites may be accessed and often lay down rules for the use of e-mail facilities. It is important to read the acceptable use policy and make sure you follow its rules.

Summary questions ✓

1 a Explain two different ways that criminals can use the Internet to steal from people who bank or shop online.

b Describe three methods people can use to protect themselves from these criminal activities.

2 E-mail is very useful, but there can be problems such as phishing. Explain the meaning of this term and the problems it can cause for e-mail users.

3 'Social networking sites can put you at risk of identity theft.' Explain what this statement means and how you can protect yourself by behaving sensibly.

4 Describe three methods that a company can use to prevent unauthorised access to its data.

5 'A strong password will help to keep your data safe.' Discuss this statement, explaining what a strong password is and why not everyone uses them.

Activity 8.3

Acceptable use when online in schools

In small groups, look at the acceptable use policy that applies in your school or college. For each of the rules it includes, decide whether the rule is designed to protect against inappropriate:

■ content

■ conduct

■ contact.

Do you think all of the rules are fair and reasonable? If not, which ones do you think should be changed?

Are there any rules that you think should be added?

Key terms

Acceptable use policies: AUPs are agreements that set out what users are allowed to do on an organisation's computer system.

In this chapter you will have learnt:

✔ the health risks that computer users face and what they can do to reduce them – these include spinal damage, eye strain and RSI

✔ the health and safety hazards that are present in an office environment and what can be done to prevent them

✔ how to behave safely and responsibly online

✔ some of the Internet frauds that criminals use to steal money

✔ methods of preventing unauthorised access to computer data

✔ methods of preventing fraud and theft using ICT

✔ the importance of following an acceptable use policy.

AQA Examination-style questions

1 A small fast food 'drive thru' restaurant has bought two new computers. It needs to use them to send and receive information from head office. The restaurant manager is concerned about the safety of the computers, because it would be easy for customers arriving by car to steal them.

Describe two methods of physically keeping the computers secure. *(2 marks)*

2 Which of **one** of the following would be **suitable** method of preventing employees from accessing unsuitable websites?

A   disable Internet access

B   install antivirus software

C   switch the computer off when not being used

D   use a content adviser program in the web browser. *(1 mark)*

3 A travel agency uses networked computers that are connected to the Internet to book holidays for its customers.

  (a) Security is very important and each travel agent has his or her own password.

    (i) What is meant by a *password*? *(1 mark)*

    (ii) The choice of password is very important. Give **three** pieces of advice that you would give to the travel agents about choosing a **suitable** password. *(3 marks)*

  (b) One of the biggest security problems for the travel agency comes from hackers.

    (i) Explain what is meant by a *hacker*. *(1 mark)*

    (ii) Other than the use of passwords, explain **one** other software method of preventing hackers. *(1 mark)*

AQA, June 2008

4 Daniel Chan has just started a new job as a reporter on a local newspaper. He has to choose a password to use on the newspaper's WAN. He has come up with four possible passwords, which are:

    Daniel

    ChanNews

    DC007

    Adfhi245361

  (a) The **least secure** choice from these four passwords would be Daniel. Give one reason why this would be the least secure password. *(1 mark)*

  (b) State which of these passwords would be the **most secure** and give a reason for your choice. *(2 marks)*

AQA, June 2006

5 A company sells computer games on the Internet.

  (a) Choose **three** of the following that are advantages to the company of selling computer games online rather than from a shop.

    A   Cheaper because they do not have any staff to pay

    B   Cheaper because they get the games free

    C   Cheaper because they do not have to rent and equip a high street shop

    D   Gives them access to a worldwide market rather than a local one

    E   Gives them access to people over the age of 18

    F   Gives their customers 24-hour access. *(3 marks)*

(b) Give **two** disadvantages to the **company** of selling the games online rather than from a shop. *(2 marks)*

(c) Give **two** disadvantages to the **customer** of buying games online rather than from a shop. *(2 marks)*

AQA, June 2006

6 Online shopping for items such as food, books and CDs is increasingly becoming an everyday part of life in the 21st century.

(a) Describe possible **advantages** of online shopping to both the companies who operate it and to their customers. *(6 marks)*

(b) Describe the possible disadvantages of online shopping to both the companies who operate it and to their customers. *(4 marks)*

7 A new computer system has recently been installed into an office. Each member of staff now has a PC on their desk.

(a) Discuss possible health and safety implications of the use of computers in an office. *(5 marks)*

(b) Describe what steps can be taken to alleviate some of these problems. *(4 marks)*

AQA, June 2007

9 Collaborative working

9.1 Principles and processes of collaborative working @k!

Collaboration is when people work together to achieve a common target. There are many situations in which people need to work together to produce an end product such as an agreement, a document or a computer system. Collaborative working methods help people with a common target to produce the end product they need.

An example of working collaboratively would be the production of a school yearbook. A group of five year 11 students have decided to produce a yearbook with quotes and photographs of all the students in the year. They intend to get the yearbooks printed by a professional printing company.

All members of the team work together to plan what needs to be included and what jobs need to be done:

- All of the students in the year are to write about themselves, their hopes and ambitions.
- Jas and Amber are to take the photographs.
- Ben and Ali are to lay out the photographs and text to make the artwork to send to the printers.
- Isabel is in charge of getting quotes from printers and getting the artwork to them on time. She will also take orders for the yearbook and collect the money.

If several people are working on a document, it is important that their work is consistent in writing style and in layout. Often, a **house style** is agreed before work starts and a template is set up so that fonts, styles, margins and other layout features are easier to control. The yearbook is an informal student document, so it would probably not use the school's house style in full, but a template would ensure that each student page has the same basic layout.

Working in this way is sometimes called a **recursive** process. In this example, each person in the chain works on the document to improve and refine it until everyone is happy with the finished product. Once a draft version has been written, it will be:

- **revised**: reviewed to see whether it needs to be altered or amended for any reason and to check that it conforms to the agreed house style
- **edited**: style, word choice and grammar are checked
- **proofread**: to spot any last-minute errors.

The people involved will check the text, looking for slightly different things. Someone needs to make sure all of the students have been included and the text and photographs are applied to the correct student. Editors will make sure the text is not too long to fit in the space

Objectives

Understand that collaborative working involves groups of people, companies or countries working together.

Understand the processes that collaborative working may involve.

Know a range of situations where collaborative working may be suitable.

A *Many ICT projects involve collaborative working*

Did you know ??????

If you have ever been part of a multi-user online game, you have worked collaboratively with other gamers to achieve a common goal.

Key terms

House style: an agreed set of layout and format rules that might involve logo placement, fonts, colour schemes, etc.

Recursive: a process that is repetitive, for example where a document is revised, edited and proofread to improve the final product.

allowed for each student. Proofreaders will make final checks for errors, particularly in spelling and grammar. The head of year 11 will also want to review the book to make sure that it does not contain anything inappropriate. Each reader will suggest changes until a final version is agreed and the **artwork** is sent to the printers. Spelling and grammar checkers will be used as part of this process, but it is important to realise that these will not find all of the mistakes that may be present.

■ Collaborative working processes

Planning

One of the first jobs to do on a collaborative project is to agree a plan. The project plan shows which person is to cover each task and by what date it must be finished if the overall **deadline** is to be met. The project plan should also have **milestones** built into it. Milestones are key points that must be reached by a certain date if the project is to be completed on time. Everyone involved must keep checking to make sure they are sticking to the plan, and if the plan needs to change for any reason everyone needs to be informed.

Communication

All of the work that the year 11 students are doing needs to be organised. Regular communication between the members of the team is extremely important. ICT provides great opportunities for collaborative working, because it allows people from all over the world to communicate in many different ways. Now that it is possible to turn voices and video into digital data that can be transmitted over a communications network, many communication methods are available. Large companies have their own international networks, but most of this communication uses public communication systems and the Internet.

E-mail

E-mails are not as expensive to send as traditional posted letters, and they arrive much more quickly than a letter would. They are a very popular way of exchanging information and sending files to one or more members of a team.

Instant messaging

Instant messaging allows two or more users to have a 'conversation' in real time by typing messages to each other. They can also send files across the connection, which is particularly useful for collaborative working. Most instant messaging software now has the facility to use a microphone to add voice and a web cam to add video if the users want to. It is possible to save the conversation for future reference. Many instant messenger users like to add emoticons, tiny pictures that show smiley faces, hearts, flowers or just about anything else that would make the message more interesting.

Chat room

Internet chat also has many uses. People can log into a chat room and type messages that other people who are logged in can read and respond to. Sometimes this chat is simply social, but an increasing number of companies use chat to supply customer support. A private

Key terms

Artwork: the version of a document that is sent to a printer. It includes the text of the document, not just the pictures and photographs.

Deadline: an established date by which tasks have to be completed.

Milestones: key points that must be reached by a certain date if a project is to be completed on time.

Activity 9.1

Milestones

Write a list of tasks that would have to be done for the yearbook project. Highlight where you think the important milestones would be if the overall task is to finish on time. Bear in mind that two tasks can be carried out at the same time as long as they are being done by different people.

AQA Examiner's tip

Do not use words such as 'quicker' or 'cheaper' without explaining them. 'An e-mail is quicker' would not gain marks. 'An e-mail arrives more quickly than a posted letter' would gain marks.

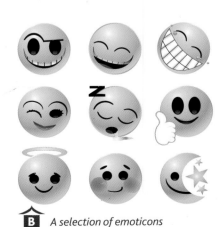

B *A selection of emoticons*

chat room is a useful way for people who are working collaboratively to discuss things without having to set up a videoconference. The students working on the yearbook project could use the group facilities of instant messaging software to discuss issues relating to the project.

Voice over Internet Protocol

VoIP (Voice over Internet Protocol) is a way of using an Internet connection to transmit the sound of voices. That means that it can be used to make telephone calls without paying the telephone company for each call that is made. For users with broadband connections, VoIP calls are essentially free. A microphone and speakers can be used, but it is also possible to buy VoIP phones and mobiles.

VoIP technology can cut down on mobile-phone bills. Both people involved in the call have to be using VoIP for this to work. Skype is one example of using VoIP technology, and it can be used for free Skype-to-Skype calls on Internet-connected mobile phones.

Activity 9.2

Communication

Draw up a table of all the methods of communication that the yearbook team could use. For each method, you must explain why they might choose to use it and what information they might pass on using that method.

Project management

All projects need:

- an agreed list of tasks showing who is responsible for each one
- a clear **schedule** of when each task must be completed
- a list of **resources**, such as hardware and software, that will be needed for each task
- an agreed **budget** that must be kept to
- a method of managing it, such as project management software
- a final deadline for the completion of the project.

The bigger the project is, the more important it becomes to plan and manage it efficiently. **Project management software** can be used to help project managers track the progress of the project. The information about each stage can be viewed in different ways. **Gantt charts** are often used to display the time schedule for each task and to show whether the work is on time. If one task is falling behind, the chart will show the effect that it might have on the finishing time of the whole project.

Workflow management software allows an organisation to set up systems where data is passed on to the people who need it within the project. Each team member can fill in forms giving the data that is needed automatically to the people who need it. This helps managers to track the progress of projects and to model the effect of any delays. It might help them to make decisions. For example, they may decide that they need to put more people on to one part of a project to avoid it delaying progress further down the line.

Key terms

VoIP: Voice over Internet Protocol, a method of using internet technologies to make phone calls.

Schedule: a time plan listing all of the tasks in the project and when they must be completed.

Resources: things that are required for the project, for example hardware, software, or even people with specialist skills.

Budget: a financial plan to show how much money can be spent on each part of the project.

Project management software: a computer program to help plan projects and resources.

Gantt charts: diagrams that show a schedule of individual tasks as they occur over the period of time during which the project is developed.

Workflow management software: a computer program to help a business manage the flow of a project.

Remember

You will be able to discuss communication methods better in an exam if you have used them. You may have used instant messaging or chat before, but why not set up a videoconference with a friend.

Project Development Schedule

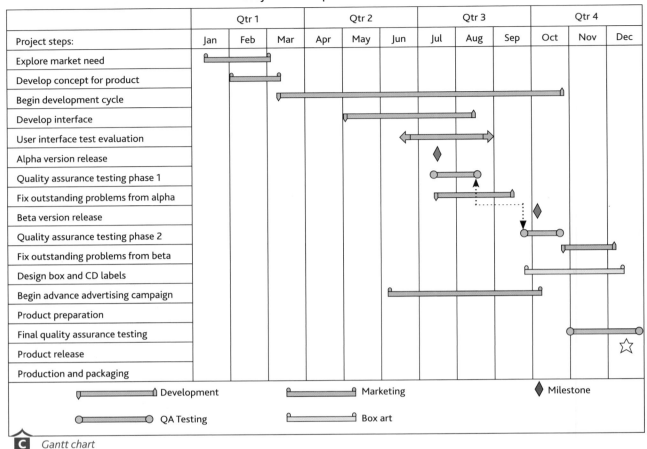

Project steps:	Qtr 1			Qtr 2			Qtr 3			Qtr 4		
	Jan	Feb	Mar	Apr	May	Jun	Jul	Aug	Sep	Oct	Nov	Dec
Explore market need												
Develop concept for product												
Begin development cycle												
Develop interface												
User interface test evaluation												
Alpha version release												
Quality assurance testing phase 1												
Fix outstanding problems from alpha												
Beta version release												
Quality assurance testing phase 2												
Fix outstanding problems from beta												
Design box and CD labels												
Begin advance advertising campaign												
Product preparation												
Final quality assurance testing												
Product release												
Production and packaging												

Development   Marketing   Milestone

QA Testing   Box art

C *Gantt chart*

■ Working within a team

When people work as a team on a joint product they have to get used to the fact that other people will review and criticise their work. Members of a good team trust each other to criticise in a positive way so that the end product gradually gets better as each person contributes. Constructive criticism makes you look at your own work more closely, it gives you ideas and helps you to make the next piece of work better.

Members of the team need to communicate with each other on a regular basis so that everyone is kept up to date with the progress being made. Sometimes this will be by telephone, e-mail or instant messaging, but at other times a more formal meeting will be needed. Usually, meetings are planned in advance so that everyone can fit them into their work schedule. There may also be times when emergency meetings are needed because a problem has cropped up. The things that are going to be discussed at the meeting are listed in the form of an agenda. This is given to people in advance so that they have time to think about the points they might want to make. The discussions that take place and the conclusions that are reached are written up as the minutes of the meeting.

Activity 9.3

Creating a Gantt chart

Assume the yearbook team has six weeks from starting the project to handing out the finished books. The printers need one week to do the printing. Draw a Gantt chart to plan the schedule for the project.

Activity 9.4

When do we meet?

At what stages of the yearbook project do you think there would need to be formal meetings? Add them to the Gantt chart that you created in the activity above.

Videoconferencing

Videoconferencing allows people to hold a meeting without all having to travel to one place. Each person needs a video camera and microphone to input sound and video, plus speakers and a monitor on which to see and hear the other people in the meeting. The sound and pictures are transmitted simultaneously across an Internet connection, to give a feeling that is as close as possible to a face-to-face meeting. Businesses sometimes have sophisticated videoconferencing suites, giving large, good-quality pictures. It is also possible to hold a simple videoconference using a webcam and instant messaging software to give a two-way link. The quality of sound and video will not be as good as using specialist software, but it will be less costly.

D   *Meetings can now be held using videoconferencing suites*

Videoconferencing saves time and money because team members are not required to travel to a meeting, which may also involve booking expensive meeting rooms. Reducing the amount of miles that people travel, whether by car, train or air, is also good for the environment. The arrangements can be made quickly, which makes videoconferencing particularly useful for emergency meetings. If there are files that might be discussed at the meeting, people can send these to each other electronically. It is possible to see the expressions and body language of the other people in the meeting, which helps everyone to communicate. Videoconferencing still has a less personal feeling than a face-to-face meeting and people cannot interact in quite the same way. Videoconferencing needs high bandwidth if the images and sound are to be good quality, and there is always a short time lag between one person speaking and the others hearing them. Users should remember that this is not a face-to-face meeting, and they need to ensure that they do not all talk at once.

Teleconferencing

It is also possible to hold a web-based conference using **teleconferencing** software. All of the team involved in the meeting log on at the same time. A presentation is given using a microphone and presentation software. The other members of the meeting can communicate by typing, rather like instant messaging. If they want to speak using their own microphone, they press a button to 'put their hand up', and the person running the meeting gives them permission to speak. Unlike some face-to-face meetings, this ensures that only one person can speak at a time!

Because it does not involve video, teleconferencing needs less bandwidth than videoconferencing as less data needs to be transferred.

■ Collaborative situations and software

Schools and colleges are places where collaboration can lead to a good-quality end product. Work can be submitted to teachers electronically and comments can be added to help the students improve its quality. **Virtual learning environments** (VLEs) encourage people to collaborate using **bulletin boards** and forums to discuss issues

> **Key terms**
>
> **Videoconferencing**: using ICT to hold a virtual meeting with two-way video and audio transmitted in real time.
>
> **Teleconferencing**: using ICT to hold a virtual meeting using text and sound but not video.
>
> **Virtual learning environments (VLEs)**: systems available in schools and colleges so that students can access school material from home.
>
> **Bulletin boards**: online discussion spaces where people can post messages and get responses from other people.

> AQA **Examiner's tip**
>
> Learn two advantages and disadvantages of teleconferencing and two advantages and disadvantages of videoconferencing.

> **Did you know** ??????
>
> Teleconferences can be saved so that the people involved can replay them if they need to.

that they find interesting or important. Students can work in groups, perhaps on a project, a school issue or as part of a school council.

When people work for a company, the business will use various methods to help them work together. Networks allow users to share files, and network management software allows the **file permissions** to be controlled. Some users will have full rights to a file, others may be allowed to read but not change it, and others will be allowed to read the file and change it but not to delete it. Network management software can track which users have worked on a file. This is useful when tracking changes to shared documents, especially if problems occur. Many companies have an **intranet**, which looks like a website but is only available within the company. It passes on information that employees need and may have a bulletin board where employees can discuss company issues.

Blogs, bulletin boards and forums can also be used for people's leisure time and hobbies so they can talk to other people with similar interests. Social networking sites are also used to keep members of groups in touch with each other, to post news of events and promote causes. Websites such as **www.justgiving.com** make it easy for charity fundraisers to ask their friends to help them to raise money for their favourite charities, even if they live at opposite ends of the country. **Wikis** allow people to edit and add contributions to web pages, and sites like Wikipedia are the result of lots of people collaborating. Online games sites allow people from all over the world to play games against each other or even inhabit virtual worlds where they can play a character in a huge interactive story. YouTube allows actors and musicians to connect and share their music and ideas and work together on new projects.

Collaborative documents

Most word processors have a feature on them that allows readers to add comments on the work for other people to read. They can also set the software to track changes. This means that when the work is edited, the words that have been changed appear in a different colour, and deleted words are shown with a line through them rather than vanishing altogether. Then the next person can look at the suggestions side by side with the old version and decide whether to accept the changes or not.

E *Comment balloons and track changes make it easier to keep track of changes when a document is reviewed*

Sharing files

When people work collaboratively, they will sometimes need access to the same files in order to edit them or add their comments. This needs to be controlled very carefully so that nobody works on out-of-date versions of the file. **Version control** involves agreeing how new files should be named, for example by adding a version number or date to the file name.

Example

Ben has added several entries for the yearbook from the people who wrote them and laid them out in the house style. He has saved the file as yearbook2010v1.

Jas sends a batch of edited photos by e-mail and Ali puts them in the correct places in the book. He then saves the file as yearbook2010v2.

Amber proofreads the book and finds some errors. She corrects them and saves the file as yearbook2010v3.

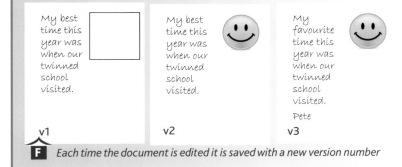

F   *Each time the document is edited it is saved with a new version number*

If you need to read the document, but you are not required to make changes to it, the document can be protected by making it read only.

One way of enforcing version control is to use a shared storage area from which the files must be accessed. The person working on the file checks it out, works on it and makes changes, then checks it back in with a new version name. A read-only version of the file remains available to other people in case they need to refer to it, but they cannot make changes to that version of the file. The storage area needs to be secure, so all of the users will need a user name and password.

Security and online safety when working collaboratively

Online security is described in more detail in Chapter 8. Students working collaboratively through a school's VLE do not have to worry much about online safety. All users of the VLE will have to register through the school, and all posts will usually be monitored so that inappropriate ones can be removed. Users should always show respect towards others. For example, forum discussions are designed to allow students to express their opinions and disagree with each other, but there is never any excuse for making rude or offensive posts. It is also important to respect the privacy of others and comply with data protection legislation. These rules would also apply to the yearbook project.

Backups

It is vital to make sure that important data is backed up so that a secure copy exists if data is accidentally corrupted or deleted. Whilst it is true that hackers and viruses can put data at risk, it is far more likely to be damaged by a hard drive failing. In a collaborative working situation, it is possible that someone will delete a file by mistake or save an old version of the file over a new one. In these situations, a backup copy is the only way to recover the data.

Backups can be made to removable media such as CD-Rs or DVD-Rs which should be labelled and stored securely, away from the main computer. Memory sticks hold a lot of data and could be used to hold a backup copy of the data. However, they are small and easy to lose or damage. Removable USB hard drives can be used, or backups can be stored online. Online backup services usually charge a fee if more than a small amount of data is stored. They make sure a copy of the data exists on their server so it is not physically close to the customer's main computer.

It is important that everyone in a collaborative working situation understands how data is to be backed up and who is responsible for doing it. If team members have files on their own computers, they must understand the need to ensure they are backed up or transferred to the central storage area.

Advantages and disadvantages of collaborative home working

Some computer networks allow **remote access** so that people can log on to them from wherever they are working. This is obviously extremely useful when people are working away from the office, but it does pose security risks as it is more difficult to be sure who is logging on.

Many people who work collaboratively work from home, a process sometimes called teleworking. This is covered in more detail in Chapter 7, pages 102–103. The biggest benefit of teleworking is not having to travel to work. This saves on time and travel costs. Teleworking benefits parents, carers and workers with disabilities in particular. It is also beneficial for someone who needs to be flexible with their time because they are working on multiple projects. There will still be some time restrictions, particularly when meetings are necessary.

Companies who employ home workers may save money as they need less office space. However, they do have to make sure they have a secure, reliable network, and arrangements must be made to ensure that work done at home is uploaded to company servers and backed up regularly.

Boost your grade!

Internet, intranet and extranet

You will be used to using web pages on the Internet, but many organisations also have an intranet. The intranet uses browser software to display pages of internal information for company employees only. Some organisations extend their intranet to customers and suppliers outside the organisation. This is called an extranet, and external users will usually have limited access rights to it. A school VLE is a form of extranet, because it allows parents as well as students to log in from home and find information they need.

Key terms

Remote access: the ability for users to log on to a network from locations outside the building where the network is.

Case study

Collaborative working from home

This book is an example of collaborative working from home. The authors wrote their material at home, uploading it to a central storage space called an e-room. The editors, reviewers and proofreaders checked the files out of the e-room, added their comments and then checked them back in again.

Summary questions

1 The students making the yearbook are working as a team.

   a Give two benefits of using a team of people rather than just one to work on a project such as the yearbook.

   b Give one drawback of using a team of people rather than just one to work on a project such as the yearbook.

2 Look closely at the pages of this book. What features of it make up its house style?

3 The text below is part of Sean's yearbook entry. There are 10 spelling and grammar mistakes.

   a Find the 10 mistakes.

   b Which mistake or mistakes would be picked up by running a spell check?

   c Which words are spelled incorrectly but would not be picked up by a spell check? Why does the spell check not find these errors?

   d The remaining mistakes are grammatical ones. List them and state which you think would be picked up by a grammar check.

> Pete and me had a grate time last summer when we went to Dublin. I had never been to Island before and I didn't no what to expect. Peat has an auntie who lives their and she let us stay at her her cottge. We was going again this June, but now we are not sure if we can afford it.

4 Give two reasons why it is important to have a clear schedule and project plan when working on a collaborative project.

5 A team is working from home at different locations all over the UK and the USA. They all have up-to-date computer equipment with microphones, web cams and speakers.

   a Give two reasons why they might choose to use videoconferencing rather than hold a face-to-face meeting.

   b Why will the team have to think very carefully about what time of day to hold the conference?

   c Give one disadvantage of holding a teleconference rather than a face-to-face meeting.

6 Many people use e-mail when working as part of a group. Describe three other ways in which the Internet can help people working together on collaborative projects.

7 It is extremely important that data does not become lost or damaged. Describe three risks to data when working on collaborative projects and explain what the group members can do to reduce the risks.

In this chapter you will have learnt that:

✔ collaborative working involves people working together to reach a common target

✔ naming files appropriately, version control and file security are important in collaborative working

✔ project management sets milestones that can help to keep collaborative projects on schedule

✔ ICT helps collaborative workers to communicate, for example through e-mail, videoconferencing, teleconferencing, instant messaging, Internet chat and VoIP

✔ collaborative working from home can save time and money because employees do not have to travel to work.

AQA Examination-style questions 🔊

1   Which **one** of the following **best** describes collaborative working?
   A   Working by yourself to set and meet targets
   B   Working all weekend to meet a deadline
   C   Working with others to meet common targets
   D   Working part-time in an office to meet your current requirements   *(1 mark)*

2   Which of the following is a **disadvantage** of video conferencing as a means of collaboration?
   A   Need to spend money on office space
   B   Need to spend money on broadband connection
   C   Need to spend money on new staff
   D   Need to spend money on travel   *(1 mark)*

3   Which is the best method for an employee to keep in touch with the company's offices, both in this country and around the world?
   A   Bulletin board
   B   Chat room
   C   Sat-nav
   D   Smart phone   *(1 mark)*

4   **(a)** What is meant by a *software tool*?
       A   A gadget that can be attached to a computer.
       B   A gadget for cleaning computer keyboards.
       C   A program used for development.
       D   A program used for car maintenance.   *(1 mark)*
   (b) A *shared workspace* is a software tool that can help collaboration. Explain how it can be used by two authors who are working to produce a book for schools.   *(2 marks)*
   (c) Describe two other software tools that can be used to assist collaboration.   *(4 marks)*

5   A rock musician in the USA and a classical pianist in the UK are collaborating on a score for a new film. Both musicians have recently installed a computer system that has Internet access. What are the possible advantages **and** disadvantages of Internet access to the musicians in collaborating on the film score? Explain your answer with reference to collaborative working processes, sharing information and teleconferencing.

   Note: You will be marked on your ability to use good English, to organise information clearly and to use specialist vocabulary where appropriate.   *(8 marks)*

Appendix

■ Generic features of GUI

Feature	Description
Icon	A picture representing a program or an operation such as Print.
Icon size	Icons can be made smaller (perhaps for a laptop) or larger to make them easier to see.
Menu	A list of options for the user to choose from. These will be grouped together to make them easier to find. For example, the Insert menu might let you insert a shape, a picture or a table.
Submenu	Some menus will bring up other menus when items are clicked. These are called submenus. For example, the Insert Picture menu might let you choose between a picture file and a piece of clip art.
Pointer	This can be an arrow shape or an 'I' shape when working with text. It can be used to show where you are in a document, or to select items from menus or click on menus.
Buttons	Icons can be drawn to look like buttons that can be pressed by clicking the mouse. Buttons are often used for navigation on websites.
Hyperlinks and hotspots	These link to other pages in the document or website which load when clicked. They can be attached to text or pictures.
Window	A window will open for each software package or document that you have open.
Close	Each window will have an icon that looks like an 'X'. Clicking the icon closes the window.
Minimise	The minimise icon will hide the window without closing it completely.
Maximise	The maximise icon will make the window as big as the screen that displays it.
Restore	Clicking on a minimised window will restore it to its normal size.
Re-size	Dragging the corner of the window will make it larger or smaller.
Toolbar	A group of icons that are linked in some way. A graphics package might have a palette toolbar, a fill toolbar and a layers toolbar for example.
Scroll bar	This is used when the display is too big to fit on the screen all at once. Moving the scroll bar changes the portion of the screen that is displayed, moving it up or down, left or right.
Dialogue box	This allows you to enter information that the computer needs, for example the number of copies to print.
Drag and drop	Using the pointer, objects and windows can be moved to new positions. Drag and drop can also be used to move text in a document or sections of a sound wave in sound editing software.
Screen resolution	The number of dots of colour (pixels) displayed on the screen, for example 1,280 × 800. High resolutions will give more detailed display, but icons will appear smaller.
Desktop contrast	High-contrast colours on the display can make it easier for people with visual impairment to see items on the screen.
Adjust volume	This makes system sounds louder or quieter.
Set date and time	You can set the date and time depending on where in the world you are situated. Most systems update the time automatically when British Summer Time starts and ends.

◼ Input devices

Device	Description
Joystick	This is mainly used by games players to control the game's movement. The joystick has a button for firing as well as a stick for moving around.
Tracker ball	A tracker ball is a bit like an upside-down mechanical mouse. The ball is on the top surface and you roll it with your fingers. It needs less space than a mouse and can be easier for people with disabilities to use.
Touch pad	This is usually found on a laptop computer, where it takes the place of the mouse as it takes up less space. You stroke the pad with your finger to control the cursor.
Scanners	These are used to convert paper-based pictures and documents into computer images. A beam of light senses the colour of each dot in the picture and builds up the image. The resolution of the image is measured in dots per inch (dpi). High dpi settings give a better image, but create larger file sizes. Colour scans create larger files than black-and-white or greyscale images.
Remote controls	Devices such as TVs and DVD players are often operated by remote controls. These use infrared beams to send signals to the device they are operating.
Interactive white board	This is a combination of a touch screen and a digital projector. The projector displays an image from the computer on the screen. You can then touch the screen to move the cursor. Some whiteboards allow you to use your finger to do this. Others use special devices that look like pens that can be used to write or highlight text.
MIDI instruments	MIDI stands for musical instrument digital interface. This type of interface is used to link realistic electronic instruments to the computer. This means that a composer can write music by playing on a midi keyboard. They can then use software to edit that music and print it out as a musical score. Tracks for different instruments can be recorded individually and then added together at a mixing desk. So one person can play several instruments and sing as well if they want to. The final product will play back all of the tracks together.
Graphics tablet	A graphics tablet works in a similar way to a touch screen. You use a stylus, which looks a bit like a pen, to draw on a flat surface. The surface senses the position and pressure of the pen and produces a matching shape on the screen. Artists and designers find it a much more natural way to draw.

◼ Generic features of applications software

Feature	Description
Print screen	This copies what is on the screen to the clipboard.
Help	This provides assistance on how to use the applications software. The Help library can be installed on your computer, and it can also be found online.
Entering and formatting text	
Select	Highlight an area, word or image on a page in order to edit it.
Text font type	Font type means the text style. Arial and Times New Roman are examples of common fonts.
Text style (emboldening, italic, underlining)	Style relates to whether the text is in bold, is italic or underlined. There are also many other styles such as strikethrough and superscript.
Text size	Size is usually measured in points. Paragraph text is typically between 8 and 12 points.
Copy, cut and paste	Copy: copies the current selection to the clipboard. Cut: copies the current selection to the clipboard then deletes the selection from the document. Paste: inserts the contents of the clipboard.
Undo and redo	Undo: undoes the most recent action. Redo: redoes what has just been undone.

Find and replace	Find: finds a particular word within a document.
	Replace: finds all instances of a particular word and replaces them with a different word or words.
Zoom	Changes the size of the document on your screen for easier viewing.
Drag and drop	Items that are selected can be dragged and dropped using the mouse.
Print and print preview	Print: sends the document to a printer.
	Print preview: shows you what the printed document will look like prior to printing.
Page layout	
Margins	Set the space between text and the edge of the paper.
Headers and footers	The contents of the headers and footers appear on every page within a document. Headers appear at the top of the page, footers at the bottom. Typical things to put in the headers or footers would be page numbers, document title, date, etc.
Page numbering	If you add page numbers to the header or footer, you just specify that you want a page number – you do not manually type in the page numbers.
Alignment, justification (left/right/full justification, centring)	Left justified means that text is aligned on the left of the page, and the margin on the right of the page is ragged – this is normal for paragraph text.
	Full justification means that the text is aligned on both the right and the left.
Orientation (portrait and landscape)	Which way up the paper is. Portrait is taller than it is wide – this book is portrait format. Landscape is wider than it is tall.
Page breaks	Where you force text to start on a new page.
Inserting and formatting objects	
Insert text boxes	A text box is used when you want text to stand out and be outside the perimeters of the rest of the paragraph text, for example a box of text in the margin.
Alignment (horizontal and vertical text)	You can change the direction in which text runs in a text box.
Crop images (including clip art, photo and scanned images)	Cropping is different to resizing because you actually cut off portions of the image.
Inserting clip art	Clip art is a library containing simple images that you can insert into documents.
WordArt (or similar)	A feature that produces very stylised artistic text.
Autoshapes	A library containing shapes such as stars, arrows, flowchart symbols, etc.
Shading	You can use shading around Autoshapes, images and text boxes.
Place behind and in front and wrap text	You can choose whether an image appears in front of or behind text.
	Text wrapping refers to the way in which text flows around an object on the page (such as an image).
Advanced features	
Templates	Templates are predesigned documents for specific tasks, for example a template for a fax or a letter.
Wizard	A wizard is a guide for creating a new document. A wizard guides you through a series of multiple-choice steps to accomplish a specific task.
	For example, there is a wizard that helps with the mail merge functions.

Common features of word processors and desktop publishers

Feature	Description
Edit text	In both word-processing and desktop publishing software you can enter text, change it or delete it.
Columns	When you open a new document, it will always appear with just one column. You can select a portion of text and change the number of columns, and text will automatically flow down the first column and into the next.
Spelling and grammar checker	These tools are important for checking accuracy. However, there are many mistakes that they will not recognise, so you should always read your work as well as using the spelling and grammar checker.
Auto wrap	Wrap refers to the way that text flows on a page. Auto wrap means that the text will automatically flow onto the next line without you needing to press Enter.
Indentation, tabs, paragraphs	Indentation allows you to select a paragraph of text and move the left edge of the text to the right. This can be a useful presentation tool.
	Tabs move the cursor a predetermined distance. Tabs are used where you want words on a line spaced at regular intervals. Do not use the space bar to try and space out text on a line.
	A paragraph is a continuous flow of text. A new paragraph begins when you press the Enter key.
Bullets, numbering and sub-numbering	Bullets are used for lists and are a very useful layout tool. You can edit the shape and size of bullets.
	Formatting a list as a numbered list means the software will automatically keep track and add the correct number when you enter a new line.
	Sub-numbering allows you different levels of numbering – for example 1 a, b, c, 2 a, b, c, etc. In a numbered list, when you press tab a sub-numbered list will be started.
Borders	These can be used to draw a box around parts of the text. You can change the border style (solid line, dotted line, etc.), border thickness and colour.
Grouping, ungrouping	If you have a number of objects that you want to move around together you can group them. When you click on one item in a group, the whole group is selected.
Layering	This is the order in which objects are placed on a page. You can change the order of the layers by using the arrange command, which lets you move objects to the front, back, etc.
Word count	This is a tool that shows you the total number of words in a selection or in the whole document.
Page and line breaks	A page break is when you force text to start on a new page. A line break is inserted by pressing Enter and forces text to start on a new line (and begin a new paragraph).
Line spacing	Line spacing means the vertical space between two lines of text. Single line spacing is normally used, but you can change this. For example, changing the line spacing to double (or 2) will insert more space between the lines of text.
Sections/chapters	If you want to format different parts of a document in different ways you may need to add a section break. Examples of format changes that require section breaks are: margins, paper size and orientation, headers and footers and text direction.
Tables, merge and split cells	You can use tables to present both text and numbers, and you can also insert images into table cells. You can also merge and split cells in a table to make the layout more flexible.

Presentation software features

Feature	Description
Insert slide	Add a new slide to a presentation.
Enter and edit text	Type in slide titles and content, edit text fonts and sizes.
Insert pictures	Insert photos, diagrams, images, etc. onto a slide.
Insert buttons	Add buttons to slides that perform actions, such as 'Go to slide 3', or play a sound.
Create hyperlinks	Make links on a slide that connect to other slides, to a document on your computer, or to a page on the Internet.
Edit layouts	Move text and images on a slide.
Change colour schemes	There are many preset colour schemes to choose from.
Slide transitions and timing	A transition is the way that one slide changes to another – for example, does the next slide fade in or dart in from the side? There are many different effects to choose from. Timing means how long each slide is displayed and how long the transition from one slide to another takes.
Animation	Animation makes objects or text move around on a slide.
Sound effects	These can be used for slide transitions or interactive buttons.
Print handouts	Print out copies of a slideshow in the form of handouts. You can select which slides to include in the handout and how many slides are printed on each page.
View slide show	Run the presentation as a full-screen slideshow.
Generic features	You also need to be familiar with a range of generic features as previously discussed, such as clip art and text styles.

Website design applications software features

Feature	Description
Template and master page	A template or master page contains all items that appear on every page in a website, such as the menu.
Hotspot	An area of a page that changes when the mouse hovers over it or clicks it. A hotspot can be invisible until you hover the mouse over it.
Adding new pages	Allows you to add extra pages to the website you are creating.
Linking pages	Using hyperlinks and hotspots to link all of the pages in a website.
Converting to HTML	Whichever web design software you use, you can convert each page into HTML code.
Publishing on the Internet	Uploading a website to the Internet.
DTP styles	These specify various details such as text font and size.
Including flash animation	Using Flash to add animated elements to a web page, such as moving objects, flashing menu items, photo rotation, animating objects when the mouse rolls over them, etc.
Counters	A website counter shows the number of visitors to that site.
Marquee	A small area of a web page that contains scrolling text.
RSS feed	RSS stands for 'really simple syndication' or 'rich site summary'. RSS feed is often included on websites to display frequently updated content (such as news headlines, share prices and blog entries) in a set format. This may include a brief summary with a link to more information.

■ Graphics manipulation software features

Feature	Description
Pick colour and fill with colour	The Pick Colour tool is used to select the current colour. The current colour will be applied to whatever you draw next.
Pencil, brush and airbrush tools	These tools each produce a different style of line. The pencil tool gives a simple line, the brush tool can take on many different shapes and sizes, and the airbrush tool produces a spray effect.
Shading	You can add shading to an object. This can be done manually or by using a built-in shading tool.
Enter text	Graphics packages are normally used for drawings, but they also allow you to add text labels or paragraphs of text.
Straight lines and curves	As well as simple straight lines, you can also draw complicated curves. You add points and the graphics package will draw a smooth line between all of the points.
Layering	You can add different layers to a drawing. This is useful if two objects overlap and you want to change which appears on top.

■ Sensors

Sensor type	Physical quantity being measured
Thermometer	Temperature
Light sensor, or LDR (light-dependent resistor)	Light
Transducer	Pressure
PIR sensor (passive pyroelectric infrared sensor)	Movement
Radiation sensor	Nuclear radiation
Wind-speed sensor	Wind speed
Humidity sensor	Humidity
Microphone	Sound
O_2 sensor, CO_2 sensor, CO sensor	Gas sensor – for example, oxygen, carbon dioxide, carbon monoxide
pH sensor	pH (acid/alkali level)

Glossary

A

Absolute cell reference: the actual location of the cell is stored, and is unaffected by the location of the cell containing the formula.

Acceptable use policies: AUPs are agreements that set out what users are allowed to do on an organisation's computer system.

Actuators: devices that perform an action in response to a signal from a computer.

Analog signals: electrical signals that vary continuously.

Applications software: computer programs that are designed to carry out specific tasks.

Artwork: the version of a document that is sent to a printer. It includes the text of the document, not just the pictures and photographs.

ATM: automated teller machine. Allows bank customers to check their accounts and deposit and withdraw money. They are sometimes called cashpoints or hole-in-the-wall machines.

Avatar: a picture that you choose to represent yourself online. It is safer than using a real picture of yourself.

AVERAGE: a function that returns the average of a set of values.

B

Backups: copies of data stored in case the original is stolen or becomes corrupt.

Biometric: using human characteristics such as fingerprints as identification methods.

Boots up: when the computer is switched on, it automatically performs a set of processes to allow the computer to be used.

Budget: a financial plan to show how much money can be spent on each part of the project.

Buffers: temporary storage areas in the printer that hold the data waiting to be printed.

Bulletin boards: online discussion spaces where people can post messages and get responses from other people.

C

CAD: computer-aided design. Uses a computer to produce drawings of the design of a product. It may also be used for automatic calculation of weights, strengths, etc.

CAM: computer-assisted manufacture. Often uses output from CAD packages. It uses computers to control the tools that manufacture or assemble products.

CCTV: closed-circuit television. An unmanned, remotely mounted video camera system is used to transmit live pictures back to a television screen where developments can be monitored and recorded.

Chain e-mails: e-mails that encourage you to make lots of copies and send them to everyone in your address book, making the chain longer. Sometimes they threaten that bad things will happen if you break the chain. They should be deleted or shown to an adult.

Client: the person who wants the new system.

Closed questions: questions where the answers are limited and the response has to be one of the options given.

Control software: software used to programme robots and devices with instructions so that they can act remotely or automatically.

Copyright: a legal right given to someone who creates documents, pictures or music.

It means that other people cannot use that work without the permission of the copyright owner.

Corrupt: the data in a file is unreadable. This can happen if the data is changed or damaged in some way so that it cannot be loaded by the original software.

CPU: central processing unit; the part of the computer that does most of the data processing.

Cyber bullying: using computers and mobile phones in ways that make another person unhappy or uncomfortable.

D

Data: raw figures or words with no context or meaning.

Databases: collections of data or records stored in tables.

Data controller: the person in an organisation who is responsible for ensuring the Data Protection Act 1998 rules are followed.

Data Protection Act 1998: a law designed to protect the privacy of personal information.

Data redundancy: when the same data is stored more than once in a table. This is sometimes called data duplication.

Data subjects: people about whom data is stored.

Data types: descriptions of the types of data being stored in a cell, for example text, numbers or dates.

Data users: people or organisations that store personal data.

Deadline: an established date by which tasks have to be completed.

Desktop publishing: also known as DTP. A type of applications software used to create printed materials containing text and images.

Devices: pieces of hardware. For example, a monitor is an output device.

Digital signals: signals that take on only two values, off or on, in binary code.

Dongle: a small piece of hardware that connects to a computer's USB port. It allows a computer user to use certain pieces of software. Most wireless broadband services use dongles as part of their modem devices.

E

E-commerce: uses the Internet for commercial tasks such as selling goods or services.

Encoding: replacing data with a code which shortens it (for example, replacing male with M or female with F).

Encryption: scrambling data to make it secure. Only users with the key to the code can unscramble and read the data.

Exemptions: situations where the data protection rules do not apply.

Export: preparing a file that is currently open so that it can be opened in different applications software.

F

Feasibility study: an investigation to decide whether it is worth proceeding with a project or not.

Feedback: the way the output influences the input. For example, a heater switching on will affect the temperature input.

Fields: column headings in database tables. Fields are part of a record.

File extension: a code that defines the type of file. At the end of the file name there is a dot plus the extension, for example letter.doc is a document file called letter.

File path: an address for the file that specifies exactly which folder it is stored in.

File permissions: the actions that users are allowed to perform on a file, for example read only or read/write.

Filter: in graphics software, a filter is a process that changes the appearance of an image. Filters are used to create specific effects, for example blur, pixelate and add brush strokes.

Firewall: software or hardware that limits the data that can be sent to or from a computer, preventing unauthorised access.

Flaming e-mails: e-mails containing angry or abusive messages.

Flash: applications software used to add animation and interactivity to web pages.

Flat file database: a database with just one table of data.

Forum: sometimes called a message board. An online discussion website consisting of user-generated content.

Functions: mathematical operations performed on the value in a cell, for example SUM and AVERAGE.

G

Gantt charts: diagrams that show a schedule of individual tasks as they occur over the period of time during which the project is developed.

Generic features: features that appear in many different types of applications software.

Grooming: a criminal offence where a person gradually builds up a young person's confidence online. They may then ask the young person to meet them in person.

GUI: graphical user interface with windows, icons, menus and pointers.

H

Hacking: accessing a computer system you are not authorised to use. Hacking is an offence under the Computer Misuse Act 1990.

Hardware: the physical objects that make up a computer system, such as computers, monitors and printers.

Hotspots: areas of a page that change when the mouse hovers over or clicks on them. A hotspot can be invisible, for example an area of an image that does not immediately look as if it is clickable.

House style: an agreed set of layout and format rules that might involve logo placement, fonts, colour schemes, etc.

Hyperlinks: links to other web pages or files, usually accessed by clicking on a word or image.

I

Identity theft: gathering personal information that can be used to identify someone, then obtaining money or goods by pretending to be that person.

IF: an IF statement asks a question, then returns one value if the answer is yes, and another if the answer is no.

Import: transfer a file that was created in one applications software package into the applications software that is currently open.

Information: data with meaning.

Information Commissioner: the government department that enforces the Data Protection Act 1998.

Input: data entered into a system. Examples of inputs are bar-codes scanned in a supermarket, or key strokes entered by a typist.

Instant messaging: real-time text conversation between two or more people who are all online.

Integrated entertainment systems: systems that combine a range of devices offering visual, musical, video, audio and gaming entertainment.

Intellectual property: ideas or creations such as software or music that can be protected by copyright.

Interactive presentation: a presentation that is affected by user input, for example the clicking of a button.

Internet fraud: a general term for using the Internet to steal money by obtaining banking or credit card details.

Internet service provider (ISP): a company that provides people with access to the Internet, for example using dial-up, cable or a broadband connection.

Intranet: a system within an organisation that looks like a website and allows people to access information.

J

Junk mail: also known as spam; e-mails that are not welcome or solicited and are often sent in bulk. Typically they are of a commercial nature.

K

Key field: also called primary key. A field in a table which uniquely identifies each record in that table.

L

Laptops: also called notebooks. A personal computer that is small enough to use on your lap and to carry around. They have a built-in keyboard, mouse and screen.

Levels of access: the rights that you have over network files.

Local Area Network (LAN): a network connecting computers in the same area/room/building.

Logging interval: the length of time between recording each measurement.

Logging period: the total length of time that data is being recorded.

M

MAX: a function that returns the largest value in a set of values.

Menu user interface: an interface where the user chooses from a restricted list of options.

Microprocessor: a silicon chip that contains a central processing unit, which acts as the 'brain' of a computer.

Milestones: key points that must be reached by a certain date if a project is to be completed on time.

MIN: a function that returns the lowest value in a set of values.

Modem: electronic device used to connect computers via a telephone line. It converts digital data to analog and vice versa.

Multimedia: content that has many different forms, such as a combination of text, audio, still images, animation and video.

N

Number formats: descriptions of how the data in a cell is displayed, for example number of decimal places.

O

OCR: optical character recognition. This can involve scanning a printed document and converting each letter shape to a text character. It can also involve a form where the user writes one letter in each box, for example in a passport application.

OMR: optical mark recognition. The data is entered by the user shading in boxes on a printed sheet. An example would be answer sheets for multiple-choice exams.

Open questions: questions where the person can give any answer at all.

Operating systems software: controls and manages the computer. Examples are Windows, Mac OS and Linux.

Output: the action that occurs after an input has been processed. For example, the name and price of an item is displayed on a monitor following a bar-code scan.

P

Passwords: combinations of letters and numbers that control access to your user name. Passwords should be kept secret.

Patch: a piece of code that updates a software package. Patches are often downloaded from the software company's website.

Peer-to-peer site: also called a P2P site; a website where people upload music and video so that other people can download it, usually illegally.

Performance criteria: statements of what levels of performance the finished product should have. An example might be that a web page must link to another specified web page.

Phishing: sending e-mails that pretend to be from a bank or organisation that handles financial transactions, asking users to click on a website link and enter banking information such as passwords.

PIN: personal identification number. A numeric password often used to access ATMs and bank accounts.

Plagiarism: copying a piece of writing, music or other intellectual property from someone else and presenting it as your own work.

Play list: a list of songs selected from a library.

Plug-in: a small software application that you download using an Internet browser. Each plug-in enables a specific feature or function of the web browser. An example would be a website containing Flash. It would offer an Adobe Flash plug-in on the site to enable you to view the Flash objects.

Podcast: audio and video files downloaded from the Internet, normally updated daily or weekly.

Presentation software: software that is used to create slideshows. Text, graphics, video and sound can be used.

Processing: turning the input into a useful form. For example, comparing bar-code data with a database to analyse which item it corresponds to.

Project management software: a computer program to help plan projects and resources.

R

RAM: random-access memory.

Records: these are also rows in a database table, and they hold all of the information about one subject.

Recursive: a process that is repetitive, for example where a document is revised, edited and proofread to improve the final product.

Relational database: a database containing two or more tables that are linked to each other. This overcomes problems of data redundancy, resulting in fewer entry errors and reduced storage space.

Relative cell reference: where the program does not actually store the address of the cell. Instead it stores the position of the cell relative to the cell containing the formula.

Remote access: the ability for users to log on to a network from locations outside the building where the network is.

Resolution: measures how many dots of colour an image is made up of. This can apply to a bitmap image, a display on a monitor or a printed page. High resolution (more dots per inch) gives better quality.

Resources: things that are required for the project, for example hardware, software, or even people with specialist skills.

ROM: read-only memory.

RSI: repetitive strain injury, a condition that causes painful joints in the wrist or fingers. It is sometimes called upper limb disorder. Using a computer for long periods of time can cause RSI.

S

Sample size: the number of questionnaires that are given out.

Schedule: a time plan listing all of the tasks in the project and when they must be completed.

SIM card: subscriber identity module card; a small electronic card inserted into a mobile phone that provides a unique ID for that phone.

Smart mobile phones: also called smart phones, PDAs or palmtops. These mobile phones offer features found on personal computers, such as Internet access, e-mail and some applications software.

SMS: short message service; a system for sending text messages on mobile phones.

Social networking: contacting other people/friends to arrange to meet or to find out about their interests.

Software licence: a legal agreement stating how a piece of software may be installed and used.

Spam filters: software that redirects e-mails that appear to be junk mail or spam into a designated junk mail or spam folder.

Spreadsheets: documents that store data in a grid of rows and columns. They allow the data to be analysed using formulae and calculations.

Spyware: software that is downloaded onto a computer without the owner's knowledge or permission. It sends data back from the owner's computer.

Stored: information is kept for later use, for example information on the stock levels after the item has been scanned.

Streaming: multimedia content is played back to the end user whilst it is still being downloaded.

SUM: a function that adds together all numbers specified in a list or range.

T

Task specific: applications software is task specific. It has a number of features that are designed to carry out particular jobs.

Teleconferencing: using ICT to hold a virtual meeting using text and sound but not video.

Teleworking: working from home using a networked computer rather than travelling to a place of work each day.

Turtle: a small robot, either real or on-screen. Simple instructions are used to programme it to move around.

U

Uniform resource locator (url): another name for a web address.

UPS: uninterruptible power supply. This protects a computer if the power fails by providing power until the computer can be closed down safely. It will also protect against voltage surges.

User: the person who will actually use the system.

User interface: the way the user interacts with the computer – input and output devices as well as the screen display.

User names: unique names that you must use to access networks.

V

Validation: ensures that data is sensible in the context in which it is being used. For example, a percentage mark for an examination must not be less than 0 or more than 100.

Version control: a system put in place to make sure that people working collaboratively do not use old versions of a document by mistake.

Videoconferencing: using ICT to hold a virtual meeting with two-way video and audio transmitted in real time.

Virtual learning environments (VLEs): systems available in schools and colleges so that students can access school material from home.

Viruses: pieces of computer code that can reproduce by copying themselves to other files. They can cause damage to stored data or stop programs running properly.

VoIP: Voice over Internet Protocol, a method of using internet technologies to make phone calls.

W

Web browser: also called an Internet browser. It is a software application used to view web pages.

Web logs: usually abbreviated to blogs. These are websites where people or organisations write entries about recent events or on a particular subject.

Wide Area Network (WAN): a network that covers a geographical area larger than a single building; it may be national or global.

Wikis: web pages that allow people who read them to edit and add content to them.

Wireless Application Protocol (WAP): a technology that allows mobile-phone users to view phone-friendly versions of websites on a phone screen.

Word processor: a type of applications software used to create text documents.

Workflow management software: a computer program to help a business manage the flow of a project.

World Wide Web (www): a system of Internet servers that support a collection of web pages on the Internet which hyperlink to each other.

WYSIWYG: an acronym for 'what you see is what you get'. It is a term used to describe software that allows the user to view something very similar to the end result while the document is being edited.

Index

Key terms and their page numbers are in **bold**